Don't
LEAD BY
EXAMPLE

THOUGHTS AND ESSAYS
ON LEADERSHIP AND LIFE

THOM HAYES

ISBN: 978-1-954614-89-5 (hard cover)
       978-1-954614-90-1 (soft cover)

Hayes. Thom

Edited by: Melissa Long
Photo credit: Piper Warlick

Published by WARREN Publishing
Charlotte, NC
www.warrenpublishing.net
Printed in the United States

To Sharon (Reed) Hayes, you've revitalized me, challenged me,
and helped me to wake up, get up, rub some dirt in it,
get back in the game, and, for better or worse, tell the story.
You are my rock (and roll).

Thanks for all you do!

"Please tell me how you lead by example."

"I don't. I lead with intention and *model* by example."

–THOM HAYES

The cave you fear to enter holds the treasure you seek.

–JOSEPH CAMPBELL

TABLE OF CONTENTS

INTRODUCTION

When I was promoted to my first corporate leadership role, I naïvely said to my mentor, "Now that we are peers, how about grabbing a drink sometime?"

She astutely said, "In three months. Then we'll have something to talk about."

It was the *experience*, not the title, that mattered.

Thirty years after that conversation, I have something to talk about, so I wrote this book for the next generation of leaders.

You are holding a book of what worked and didn't work for me.

After decades of leading people and teaching these concepts to emerging leaders to help them navigate their lives and careers, I decided to write this book. Far too often, we as leaders fall prey to the notion that newer managers or associates "should have known" something, that it was "common sense." I don't know about you, but I didn't know *something* until I learned that *something*. So, why should I assume someone else would know it?

When I served with Barnes & Noble, there was a policy that booksellers could borrow hardcover books for two weeks if they returned them in saleable condition. This was a win-win situation because the employees would better know the inventory and recommend books to customers, thus resulting in more sales. Publishers loved it, booksellers loved it, customers benefited from the recommendations, and the store and company profited as a result.

One of the frustrations of senior leadership was that each store carried hundreds of business and management books. Managers had this trove of information available free at their fingertips to learn and grow. Still, few current or future leaders in the company took advantage of it. Perhaps they felt business books were boring or didn't apply to them, or if they were going to read something in their free time, it would be something they enjoyed. There are no sex scenes, wizards, or explosions in management books. So, fair warning, there are none in this book. I wrote this for current or future leaders who do not like linear and lengthy management books. I hope they can get something out of the journey and not make the same mistakes I made along the way.

You'll find, too, that I frequently and without apology toggle between business in general, retail trade, and military in this book. That is because we are people at the root of it all, be it soldiers or salespeople, wearing boots or suits.

I hope you enjoy this journey and learn something you can apply in the process.

Thom Hayes

CHAPTER ONE

DON'T ... JUST DON'T DO IT

So, basically, you're upset that they aren't
doing what you didn't tell them to do.

—THOMAS HAYES

Once upon a time, I was a training manager for a Fortune 500 retailer. This meant that I oversaw a training store where individuals formed a farm league of sorts before getting a call into the Big Show, a promotion to a store of their own. We were a good, solid team, and it was a joy to see people come up through the ranks and get promoted to store manager. There were many successes and opportunities, but each was dependent on the quality of leadership.

In one of these operations, there was a café featuring Starbucks coffee along with pastries and sandwiches. It was profitable, but there were policies and procedures the staff was not following. They were not upselling, cleanliness was not at par, and they were not following the protocol of writing customers' names on cups. During a weekly one-on-one meeting, I asked the department manager about coaching and counseling her team. She said she wasn't doing that.

"So," I asked, "how are you leading your team?"

"I lead by example," she said. "They should be able to learn by watching me."

"Hmmm," I said. "And yet, they are not doing what we agreed they should be?"

"It's frustrating that they are not doing it the way I do it."

"So, basically, you're upset that they aren't doing what you didn't tell them to do?"

"Well, when you put it that way ... ."

That's pretty much the only way to put it. You've got to state your expectations of someone concisely and include desired behaviors, metrics, and a timeline. Some refer to these as SMART goals: Specific, Measurable, Attainable, Relevant, and Time-based.

Leading is *intentional influence*. We lead with purpose, explaining our business and the tasks at hand, and what right looks like. We work to improve ourselves by actively seeking knowledge and then cascading that knowledge and intent to individuals and teams to become actionable.

Let's say your operation is struggling with payroll, and you need to find out where the problem lies. Is it in overscheduling, and if so, why? So you observe, ask, form assumptions, and challenge those assumptions until you fully understand what the problem is. Next, you get to the *why* and develop a plan of action and communicate it thoroughly, along with expectations. Then you delegate and execute.

This is contrary to how some people new to leadership roles operate. These people believe that all they need is to lead by example, and through osmosis, leaders will develop. Yet, this is passive and subject to the mindset of the intended target audience.

It is presumptuous, as it presumes the individual wants to be a leader and is looking for a career when they may merely want a job. Further, this is kind of cowardly as it avoids difficult conversations and conflict. You might as well paper your wall with success and teamwork motivational posters and hope things work out.

Some people are uncomfortable with or afraid of tough conversations. They would rather be liked than lead, so they choose a passive method and call it "leadership." And it is so commonplace, it's in our leadership lexicon, "Lead by Example." Hell, it was a mantra when I was in the military.

Here's the rub: It is a complete fallacy.

The days of employees wanting to emulate their bosses and be like them are over. That's why leadership by example doesn't work. These employees don't want to be us, yet we need them to behave in a particular manner to represent our company. The company hired them and paid them to do the job they were hired to do. That's where intentional leadership comes into play. That's where coaching and modeling reinforce the deliberate message.

The apostle Paul wrote in 1 Corinthians 9:26-27: "Therefore I do not run like a man running aimlessly; I do not fight like a man beating the air. No, I beat my body and make it my slave so that after I have preached to others, I will not be disqualified for the prize."[1] Essentially, "preached" is providing direction and intent. The modeling comes in as Paul's walk matches his talk.

1 Holy Bible 1978, New International Version. 3 I Corinthians, 9:26-27. P. 1061. Zondervan Bible Publishers, Grand Rapids, Michigan.

One can *model* by example, but one cannot *lead* by example. Leadership is an active state. It is intentional influence and instructive. The best leaders lead by showing, not telling, and they sure as heck don't do it merely by example. Modeling is passive, and it only *reinforces* what has been shown. People watch what you do as a leader, and it will be held up to you and against you at different times of your life. But you cannot expect a new employee working part-time in a job to know what you expect of them by merely modeling. That person views modeling as an *indication* of what *you* do, not what *they* are *expected* to do.

When onboarding new hires, particularly ones new to the workforce, I would begin by saying, "I hired you to do a job, not to give you a job." That sets the tone. An employee is there to provide a service or labor that is necessary for the company to function. In return, they receive pay, knowledge, and respect. I believe in dignity in all things, and it goes both ways, and while that attitude is modeled, the *why-what-how* has first to be shown, taught, and reinforced. And if you want people to excel at the job you hired them for, you must lead—but not by example.

How many of you are parents of teenagers? When you modeled cleaning your house and doing laundry or dishes, were your children inspired to do the same, to put down their phones, and say, "Hey, let me help you with that." No? That is the point here. Teens grow up to be adults and will behave the same way unless directed or led intentionally. You must begin leading them by teaching them how to do chores and providing them with the incentives to get them done, and teaching them the consequences when the work is not done—for example, the carrot (allowance) or the stick (phone forfeiture).

There is a difference between role mentor and role model. Being a mentor is intentional; being a role model is not. The reason NBA baller Charles Barkley and Nike Air partnered to produce the 1993 commercial "I am not a role model" is that people chose to model their behavior on Barkley's behavior. He was leading unintentionally because people who respected his prowess were choosing to follow his lead. Barkley didn't want that role of leadership off the court. He wanted to excel at basketball. We are talking here about people who choose to be leaders so that they can intentionally influence people.

When work is to be done, it begins with selling the vision of what successful task completion looks like. "You'll know you've done it right when 'X' looks this," for example. You prepare, tell, show, and do, then have your child or protégé review and do it on their own, and then you provide feedback. They do it not for the love of country or a parent; they do it because it was laid out as an expectation, and they were motivated by carrot or stick to do so.

And remember, whether teenage child or middle-aged new employee, you need to follow up with praise if the vision is satisfied. If it's not, then you need to coach and correct.

If you walk by someone who's not up to standard and don't correct them, you have just set a new standard.

Chapter Two

DEAL(ING) WITH IT

Major Walter Debany was a mentor of mine in the 1990s. During one Army National Guard mission in Honduras, he led a team comprised of me and one other member. Before the duty day, he and I would rise at 4:00 a.m., meet at the mess tent, grab a cup of coffee, and walk around the perimeter of the base camp to prepare our minds for the day ahead. We talked of mission, leadership challenges, relationships, finance, and whatever else came up during the 30-minute walkabout.

On one of these occasions, we spoke of how hot it was there, 115 degrees Fahrenheit at midday. I told him the soldiers were complaining about the heat. He said they were wasting time complaining about something beyond their control.

"Yes, it is hot. So now what? We still have to accomplish the mission," he said.

It was by changing our mindset and reframing that we were able to find a way to complete the mission, and we did it regardless of the environment. It was hot for everyone, not just us, so we accepted it, managed it, and moved on with it.

In their seminal work, *Designing Your Life*, authors Bill Burnett and Dave Evans describe situations beyond one's control as "gravity problems."[2] As much as you cannot change the force of gravity when riding your bicycle up a hill, you have to adjust and reframe what you're doing in response to the gravity. That was Debany's point as well; we couldn't change the environment, and we couldn't *not* accomplish the mission, so we improvised, adapted, and overcame.

Another way is to communalize the feeling by *embracing the suck*.[3] This phrase helps label the feeling and addresses the "This is bad and is not fair" mini-me ego that sometimes pops up in all of us. It's a leveling and grounding phrase that puts things in perspective and simultaneously consoles and motivates a person in a challenging situation. Misery loves company, and this phrase elevates that company from a pity party to a place of recognition that we are all experiencing a gravity problem. While we cannot change it, we can muster our strength and deal with it.

---

2 Bill Burnett and Dave Evans, Designing Your Life: How to Build a Well-Lived Joyful Life (New York: Alfred A. Knopf, 2016), 8.

3 A colloquial military phrase, such as "Welcome to the suck." It means that the place or mission sucks, and it's an acknowledgement of it. Sets expectations.

Often, we worked with local civilians, and they adapted to the environment in creative ways. On one occasion in Honduras, they fashioned hats out of paper plates to keep them cooler as they worked.

My wife likes to tell the story of a hike she went on with her son, Michael, when he was ten. Her husband at the time, knowing the rigors awaiting them on the weekend hike along with both of their temperaments, said, "There's no way you'll make it through the weekend. You guys are going to kill each other."

Sharon turned to her son en route to Grayson Highlands National Park. "Listen," she said. "We are going to get hot, tired, and hungry. There will be times when we want to quit. It's going to be hard, and it's not going to be what we expected, and we're both going to feel that way. But at that moment, we have a choice. We can either act out and take it out on one another, potentially ruining what could be an amazing weekend, or we can acknowledge that we're both going to feel that way and make a different choice."

They acknowledged the potential strain in advance—the "gravity" problems. Labeling their feelings and having figuratively built a bucket to contain them, they had a fantastic weekend, filled with happy memories to last a lifetime.

I respect people who do this, recognize the situation, and focus on managing the mission to its successful conclusion instead of being a victim. I remember an instance in the Holyoke, Massachusetts Barnes & Noble I managed. Every day, a young man came into the café and studied his schoolwork at a table ... *every day*. I commented on his work ethic to him, and he said, "I am not the smartest. I struggled in school, I have Attention Deficit Disorder, so none of this is easy for me. I know I will have to work twice as hard as everyone else to be in the same field, but I am willing to do that." I offered him a part-time job because I valued his work ethic. He accepted, did a great job, finished his studies, and became an EMT.

I doubt he stopped there.

Focus on what matters and what you can control. Everything else is just background noise.

Chapter Three

COMMUNICATING

*The single biggest problem in communication
is the illusion that it has taken place.*
—George Bernard Shaw

Sharing is caring.

I had the privilege of working under many commands during my tenure in the military. One that is striking, though, was my time during the Balkan campaign of the mid-1990s. Our unit was attached to an Army Division in Germany. In one of the command centers in Wiesbaden, there was always a hive of activity, clicking keyboards and urgent conversations.

A six-foot-long, dot-matrixed banner hanging on the wall proclaimed the following words: "WHO ELSE NEEDS TO KNOW?" These words set the tone and were put in place by a commander who recognized and insisted upon thorough communication. Nothing fell through the cracks because there was hell to pay in the way of a public dressing down and harm to reputation when it did.

If a directive had come down, moving more troops into an area of operation, many other people need to know this. This is logistics and communication. Let's say one hundred more troops are being transported to an area, which means those in charge of transportation need to know. The command's responsibility is to ensure that the troops are transported, fed, and housed. If all arrive on-site, and no one there knew they were coming, that is a huge problem.

Communication failure is the single most common avenue to defeat. The most frequently heard response to "Why didn't you tell anyone?" is that they intended to but were OBE (Overcome By Events) and forgot. Or, my favorite, "I thought they already knew." Be it change in mission, change in schedule, conveying a message that someone called and is expecting a call back, saying you will call someone back and becoming distracted by multiple tasks and events requiring immediate attention, you are simply forgetting.

Teaching and reinforcing clear communication are where senior leadership can help develop future successful leaders. The mastery of communication of intent, task, and record of said communication to avoid the inevitable "Who did you tell?" question and "I don't remember" answer when something falls through the cracks is essential. You want to ensure all stakeholders know relevant information and their responsibilities to the outcome.

I use *intent* as the *why* we are doing what we are doing. As business thought leader Simon Sinek says, "You have to start with Why." Then explain what, how, and where the individual you're explaining it to fits into the scheme of things. And back to the beginning of this chapter, who else needs to know what the objective is and decisions made around that objective?

Let's take a minute to discuss some strategies and tactics to capture and convey messages.

I know of one manager who keeps sticky notes on his fingers as he walks around, removing each as it is successfully communicated either in person or via text or email, creating an electronic chain of custody. Similarly, several others keep a record in a notebook and have a budgeted amount of time at the end of their day to ensure each item and decision is crossed off after resolution or communication. Nothing is left hanging. Frequently, I do not have the contact person's info readily available, so I email myself a reminder to notify the person, then, should I forget, it pops up in my email chain to do so. You could also email yourself a reminder to provide the recipient more details or, using your smartphone, email the person immediately.

The other side of the coin can be equally frustrating—not hearing back or the unanswered email.

"I'll get back to you." I've heard and said this many times, and the implied promise strikes me. Over the years, I've had experiences where I was left hanging, and in unpacking the why, here's what I've found:

Unanswered texts: As in, discovered text during an insomnia-fueled 4:00 a.m. text scroll and intending to reply at a more reasonable hour, then more text messages come in above it, so it gets buried and, therefore, forgotten.

Unanswered emails: Email sent made person uncomfortable or, as above, recipient wanted to put thought into a response, was subsequently overcome by events (OBE), and forgot, or intended recipient never received it because it was sent to the wrong email.

Another frequent event is the email ended up in their spam folder, their reply ended up in yours, or it was blocked by the firewall on either end. The point is not to assume the other party is ignoring you.

Unanswered projects: A deliverable to you is late, and the individual has "ghosted" you. It is likely one of the following:

1. The person doesn't know how to handle the case's specifics and is embarrassed to admit it and won't ask for help from a colleague.
2. It is difficult, and the individual doesn't know how to tackle it, so they procrastinate—*Mad How Disease.*[4]
3. The individual has personal problems and cannot properly focus on this matter—I had this happen with an attorney once.
4. Having previously given recommendations to be executed to prevent bad news, the individual doesn't want to say the bad news occurred. Many people do not like to be the bearer of bad news, so they procrastinate, making the bad news seem worse when it's announced.

The solution is to communicate early and often. In the case of unanswered emails, I've found a follow-up email sent while forwarding the previous email and stating, "Hey, I know you're swamped with emails, so I wanted to move this to the top of your inbox" is adequate.

---

4 I credit consultant Bruce Hurley for introducing this portmanteau to me, combing Mad Cow Disease with the "How" analysis-paralysis.

Ghost Busting

In the ghosting of a deliverable project, the tone should be much less conciliatory. Your ass is on the line, so you must be more direct. A follow-up email with all the previous emails in tow and cc'ing that individual's boss and anyone else expecting the deliverable will often *inspire* action.

I have a business, and it has some tax complexities. I gave my CPA end-of-year materials weeks before the April 15 deadline. He was unable to meet the deadline and filed an extension. This would be the first time in my life I would be filing late. I followed up, and on April 25, his assistant wrote me: "Bob is working on your return. It should be done within the next two weeks. Thank you." Those weeks came and went, and I was told it would be the first week of June … and then that week passed.

I never found out the reason for the delay. Once the filing finally occurred, I terminated our relationship as I could not have anyone on my team who performs like that. When you're dealing with professionals, you have the right to expect them to behave professionally. Hold your vendors accountable.

Finally, there's the need to communicate bad news promptly. I bore witness to the fallout of delaying communications. There was a department manager who was not meeting her job goals. As the store manager was about to do a negative performance counseling, the department manager's father passed away, and she was understandably upset. Feeling compassion, the store manager did not give the department manager the counseling as she thought it would be kicking her when she was down. A few months later, when the department manager did not receive a raise during her annual review, she was angry, asking why she wasn't told she wasn't meeting expectations as she and her husband were expecting a pay raise.

"Go ugly early" has been my communications modus operandi for years. Unlike wine, bad news doesn't get better with age.

Another aspect is ensuring you, as the leader, understand the message before you deliver it. You must fully comprehend what is being asked of or told to you. In a strategic sense, you have the company's mission statement, which lays out what the company stands for and why it is in business. And within those parameters—and sometimes beyond as the company evolves—there are specific subsets, jobs, or projects to be accomplished. In these, there is intent. In other words, we are doing this not to keep you busy, but because it needs to be done, and here is why—and the *why* should never be "Because I told you so."

As a recipient of the project, you must fully understand the depth and breadth of what is expected of you and your team to execute it correctly. This can be accomplished by asking the following question: "What does success look like when it is complete?" You want to ensure you have the same vision as your leaders to instill in those looking to you for guidance. Keep it simple and direct. You must know the mission intent and specifications before you deliver to the team. W. Edward Deming said, "If you can't describe what you are doing as a process, you don't know what you're doing."

There have been times when I've been out and plan to stop at the grocery store. I text my wife to tell her I am stopping there and to let me know if she needs something. Well, at the beginning, I'd receive: "Milk, cheese, bread," and I would inevitably come home with the 2 percent milk when she wanted 1 percent; cheddar cheese when she wanted Swiss, and sliced sandwich bread when she wanted French loaf for dipping. We evolved, and I learned to ask more specific, clarifying questions, and my wife learned to explain it as if to a child—which I am in a grocery store. The point is, whether filling a shopping list, holding terrain in a military operation, or doing a merchandise reset in a big-box retailer, you need to know what precisely is expected of you, and your people need to know what outcome is expected from them, what right looks like, and what success looks like. Vet your written and verbal messaging to ensure it cannot be misinterpreted.

There is also the point of knowing your audience. Not everyone thinks or feels like you do. Yes, this truth can be a brutal awakening for some, but alas, it is true. So, given that, we must know the audience with whom we are engaging. A friend relates the tale of adapting his language to better communicate with his son. Once, when the son was a teen, the father asked, "Have you thought about cleaning your room?" as a way of nicely nudging his son to clean his room. A while later, the father came back to find the state of the room unchanged. Asking his son about it, the son replied, "Well, I thought about it and decided not to." The son interpreted the comment literally, not understanding the intent. So, my friend, realizing it, adapted to a more direct approach: "I need you to clean your room."

The same holds for understanding the language. I recall a particularly cringeworthy moment when a vice president was instructing a group of managers on empowerment and navigating "the fog of war and leading *through* the ambiguity of it." One of the managers in attendance then cascaded to his bewildered management team how they needed to "lead *by* ambiguity."

We need to understand what is being asked to know what we need to do and say to convey the intent. If you can explain it to a five-year-old, you have demonstrated your understanding of the message. And, as a leader, hold your team accountable for not communicating, and the communication will improve.

Logann Foltz knows the importance of accurate and open communication. As store manager of a Sport Clips® in Winston-Salem, North Carolina, Foltz leads her tenured team with a nonhierarchal (flat) leadership style of "don't make me have to be manager." This style doesn't work for everyone, but it has proven successful in this operation, increasing employee engagement, customer retention, and sales.

"I had to learn how to talk to people and the psychology behind how people receive information. I use the 'sandwich method,' where you compliment, add a little bit of a critique, and praise. It's saying, 'This is something that I noticed. Is that something I can give you some advice on?' It's saying it in a way that they can receive it where they are accepting your criticism and then also saying, 'but you did such a great job with this! I'm really appreciating and can see all the hard work you've put in.' That conversation takes place behind closed doors. People take pride in what they do. You don't want to take away someone's confidence. You want to build confidence. Happy employees create a happy, upbeat, and fun environment for each other and their clients.

We have something at Sport Clips called the 'Heart of a Champion.' It's a formula to being a decent human being: Do what's right, do your best, and always treat others the way they want to be treated. It's the opposite of the Golden Rule, which says you want to treat people the way you want to be treated, because my background is not the same as somebody else's.

In the books I've read, and in the training I've gone through, I've learned there are three types of workplaces: Warfare, Peaceful Coexistence, and Active Mutual Support.[5] We're all about the latter. Our system

Logann Foltz

has the goals for the store in the middle. Everybody takes on a little bit of responsibility for that goal and asks, 'What am I contributing to this?' Then there are arrows going out to every person in that team, and everybody has a direct link to that particular goal with that particular person as opposed to their being a chain of command.

They can see their contribution is fruitful. We're able to make decisions on our own. I give everybody a lot of freedom, but you have to give me the courtesy of letting me know why you did something, then we can regroup, and if we need to alter that decision, we alter it, but we alter it together.

5 The "Active Mutual Support" that Logann refers to is addressed in the book *The Executive Speaks: An Executive Insider's 5 Power Speaking Secrets* by Phillip Guy Rochford, in which the author defines active mutual support as a "level of interaction that produces extraordinary results and satisfaction." Rochford states, "At this level individuals are actively engaged in supporting all other members of the organization. They come forward with observations and suggestions in a supportive, open, and candid fashion. Lincoln: iUniverse, 2005).

That first day of training, I say, 'Hey, we are here to find what you are great at and then use you to make other people great.' I understand that everybody's best is not necessarily your best, and we each have our own unique set of skills we bring to the table that makes us different. If I noticed that somebody else is really good at something, let's buddy you up with that person if that's something you feel like you struggle with. Not everybody will sit there and lay out all of their struggles, but it's finding that level of being comfortable enough to ask for help and making sure you set that tone from the very beginning.

I think the word manager has become a yucky word. I don't want to be a *manager*. I want to be a *leader*, and everybody else can also be a leader."

Chapter Four

ACCOUNTABILITY

Holding yourself and others accountable
is an act of respect, not reprimand.

—Sharon E. Reed

Great teams begin with sound individuals who produce great results together. These teams evolve into an ecosystem and, like any ecosystem, have internal and external vulnerabilities.

Personal accountability is foremost on the respect continuum.

"So, how's that working out for you?" is usually used as a snarky comment intended to make a point or to impugn someone else's decision. I use it differently because I say it to myself. It helps me refocus my priorities and hold myself accountable. I constantly reevaluate my choices. Everything we do is a choice. How we respond to factors beyond our control is a choice. I endeavor to choose wisely, and asking myself "How's that working out for me?" is a litmus test of sorts, a checking of my internal guidance system to ensure I am on the right course.

At one point, a general manager of a retail store was having difficulty holding someone accountable because he felt the individual had not been adequately trained, adding, "We have to give her the benefit of the doubt." While very noble, his team pointed out that the individual's frequent mistakes were not the product of not being trained. She had been trained and retrained.

" The culture of any organization is shaped by the worst behavior the leader is willing to tolerate. "

–TODD WHITAKER

She was simply incapable of performing her duties and unwilling to transfer to another position. She would leave cash unattended in plain view and would even leave her associates hanging because she forgot she'd said she would be back to help them. She was too scattered and frazzled to be effective. There was talk of accountability but no action toward it. Other people on the staff realized there was little consequence for nonperformance, so they didn't step up.

Another issue with the individual was low loyalty card conversion—how many non-members were "converted" into members. The store was performing dismally on her shifts.

The GM here, too, felt that coaching, not accountability, was the key. Again, very noble—though, the company wasn't paying him to be noble. It was paying him to produce results. To do so, you educate, check for understanding, reinforce, and hold the employee accountable. You change the people, or you *change* the people. In the end, the individual who was not performing well, tragically, took her own life. While there was no note left behind explaining why, in hindsight there were larger issues at play in her world. The point in sharing this is there are consequences to playing it too safe and not taking action. The store continued to fail at loyalty card conversions, and the staff continued to flounder. The GM was finally replaced.

I once dealt with a manager who felt it was her moral obligation to acquiesce to the scheduling needs of an employee versus the needs of the store. I explained that as store manager, she was letting the tail wag the dog. Good managers are fair and consistent, but their role is to develop people, grow the business, and protect assets. She had to either get the employee to change shifts or let the person go. If she didn't do that, we would put someone else in her management position and terminate her employment. Then she would be unemployed, and the person she was trying to protect would be removed anyway. That may seem harsh, but when all else fails, there is often value in shock statements such as that or "It sounds like you have a lot of challenges, let's not add being unemployed to the mix." While you want the person you're counseling to succeed, they must deliver. So long as you are fair and consistent in treating the people and the situation with dignity, you will likely succeed.

I had to engage in many situations I did not want to or did not feel comfortable doing in the military. In those dry-mouth moments, I would physically touch the rank on my collar and take solace and muscle from that. In those situations, I would remind myself, *Be the rank, not the person.* As a leader, you too will be called upon to take unpopular stances, so take comfort in your position and execute the job description. This kind of cognitive dissonance is part of the job.

I recall an instance when my unit was attached to an active Army unit in Wiesbaden, Germany. We did physical training (PT) with their unit every morning at 6:00. PT was done in company formation on an asphalt parking lot and in unison. So everyone did the same exercise simultaneously in cadence. I noticed many soldiers lying on their sides not participating because they were injured—usually from a back injury. Every day, sit-ups were done on the asphalt, and the backbone on asphalt was not a good feeling. In the testosterone-fueled environment, doing such was supposed to make you "tougher."

Having fewer people in the unit participate because the making-them-tougher method was turning into making-them-injured didn't jibe with me. So while I did it and dreaded it, I also knew it was wrong. So I calmly set about researching the regulations (Field Manual 7-22), which clearly stated that this particular exercise should be performed on a soft surface. I wrote the commander a memo citing my concern and the source document, and presented it to him. Now, keep in mind, this was not my unit commander, but the commander of the company we were attached to and, by default, who had charge over us. There was a risk of retaliation against us as a perceived "weaker" National Guard unit in a "tougher" active army environment.

The courage to stand alone is heralded, but it is also risky and a definite dry-mouth decision. In this case, the commander called me into his office, thanked me, and said I was right and he would instruct his team to change the way they conducted PT.[6] But the best part was when my active army peer, who had been one of the injured, came up to me later and thanked me for having the courage to do what he did not, thus sparing others from suffering further injury.

I did that to protect the soldiers under my charge, which is the responsibility of leadership. Holding people accountable is a part of that responsibility.

---

6 In 2020, FM 7-22 was revised, and the Army Physical Fitness Test (APFT) no longer contains sit-ups, therefore, it is not a requirement of PT.

CHAPTER FIVE

STRATEGY, TACTICS, AND EXECUTION

I'm the decider, and I decide what is best.
—GEORGE W. BUSH, 2004

The systematic management of concentrated resources, in a nutshell, is what we do as leaders.

We manage things, process, and property, and we lead people. We have a sales plan, which consists of different metrics we must attain. This is our *offense*. And we have a budget we must maintain, which is our *defense*. Like any successful sports team, we must execute both to our full potential. Leaders plan and execute. It's up to the boots (us) to achieve what the suits (C-Suite) have planned.

When I started with Barnes & Noble Booksellers in the early 1990s, the job description began with this mission statement: "To provide and ensure excellent customer service in order to maximize company sales and profits." To this day, the intent of that mission statement resonates with me as one of the most clear-cut I have encountered.

Rubber, meet the road.

President Dwight D. Eisenhower said, "War is taking any problem exactly as you take a problem in your own life, stripping it down to its essentials, determining for yourself what is important and what you can emphasize to the advantage of your side; what you can emphasize that will be to the disadvantage of the other; making a plan accordingly—and then fighting just as hard as you know how, never letting anything distract you from the prosecution of that conception."

Now, substitute the word *business* for the word *war*, and you get the idea. Read, learn, and breathe the last sentence, and you understand. To prosecute is to continue with a course of action with a view to its completion. This is how we execute. The "prosecution of that conception" is the strategy from which we get off our collective butts and take action. We commit to the plan, communicate it, execute it, and adapt as necessary along the way.

Consider the offense of a football team. They have drawn up a plan, and the quarterback, as team leader, commits to it and communicates it in the huddle. At the snap of the ball, the offense executes it, and adapts to the defense during the play.

We, as leaders, are delegated the authority to accomplish our portion of the mission. It is imperative to understand that while we can delegate authority, we cannot delegate responsibility. You are the one who is responsible for making decisions and getting things done. You are, as George W. Bush famously coined, "The decider." You must develop, commit, and execute/prosecute the plan. You are the project owner, the Project Manager, and you must be agile enough to navigate changes and ambiguity. To reach back to Eisenhower again: "Planning is everything; plans are worthless."

Command intent is more than a sound bite. It's a touchstone, the sticking place upon which to screw one's courage. Every action can be weighed against purpose. Every decision is made with the stated "intent"—the *why* we are doing what we are doing—in mind. When we approach an activity, the question "To what end?" should be asked. Is this leading us to our goal?

Everyone in the organization must be thoroughly briefed on the mission. When I was going through military leadership training, I recall one event where the instructor took the squad leader aside and told him about the task at hand. He then instructed the squad leader to come back and brief the squad. Once done, the instructor came over and "killed" the squad leader as a test to see how thoroughly he briefed us so we could accomplish the mission without him. The squad leader had informed us thoroughly, so the mission was accomplished.

In sum: Who else needs to know? In need-to-know situations, people need to know their role in the plan's execution. You accomplish this by fully understanding what is expected of you by asking clarifying questions from the person providing direction. Then you transfer that knowledge and expectation to your team and ask them to back-brief—"What is your understanding of what I need from you?" Define the parameters of who is responsible for communicating updates and how we gauge progress.

You gauge progress by measuring what matters. For example, you know where you are going, but where *are* you relative to your goal or sales plan? In the military, it was beans, bullets, bandages, and bytes. The civilian sector's supply chain, cost of goods, payroll, and other overhead leads to people, product, process, and technology. These are all input into profitability, which is why we are in business. These are the nouns that matter, the inputs that lead to sales, sustainability, and growth.

So we know the *why* and the *what*, but how do we measure what matters? Key Performance Indicators (KPIs) and Objectives and Key Results (OKRs) are two commonly used methods, and as a leader, you will have to fall into whichever of these the company employs.[7] OKRs is a godsent methodology by John Doerr in his book *Measure What Matters*.

As explained by www.WhatMatters.com authors Ryan Panchadsaram and Sam Prince: "An Objective is simply what is to be achieved, no more and no less. By definition, objectives many companies use are significant, concrete, action-oriented, and (ideally) inspirational. When properly designed and deployed, they're a vaccine against fuzzy thinking—and fuzzy execution. Key Results benchmark and monitor how we get to the objective (O). Effective KRs are specific and time-bound, aggressive yet realistic. Most of all, they are measurable and verifiable. You either meet a key result's requirements or you don't; there is no gray area, no room for doubt."[8]

What I like about this whole process is it is not an indicator so much as a predictor. In other words, if the KRs are met, the O is obtained. If X, then Y. The other component is that it is not tied to compensation the way KPIs are typically. Let me tell you why that's important. When given a challenging goal, one with carrot-and-stick implications, people will find a way to hit the

---

7 Another way, the precursor to OKRs, is MBOs. Management by Objective. The challenge with this approach is it inspires more compliance than commitment. All in all, the OKR approach works for me. You can find more information by visiting: www.whatmatters.com.

8 Ryan Panchadsaram and Sam Prince, "What Is an OKR? Definitions and Examples," Examples & Resources, What Matters, https://www.whatmatters.com/faqs/okr-meaning-definition-example/.

mark. It is a primal means of survival. They need to put food on the table, after all. Wells Fargo found this out in 2018 when a scandal broke involving their salespeople facing a great deal of pressure to open more accounts per customer. Over one million checking and savings accounts were allegedly opened without customer consent. The pressure came down the food chain, and the employees seeking to alleviate that pressure found a way to make it happen. It cost Wells Fargo millions of dollars in settlements, and perhaps more importantly, it harmed its reputation. W. Edwards Deming said it best years ago: "Whenever there is fear, you will get wrong numbers."

At Barnes & Noble, the pressure was to sell new memberships to customers instead of renewing existing memberships. Employees were rewarded through local contests for doing it and were counseled if they didn't do it. Most found a way to do it, and a great deal found that instead of renewing a membership, they could convince a customer to "just open up a new one." And, when the home office policed this by comparing unique emails, the employees countered by having customers create a new email address. This caused a great deal of discontent and had to be managed carefully.

"We must trust, then verify."

–RONALD REAGAN

New memberships were a KPI for Barnes & Noble, and cross-selling was a KPI for Wells Fargo. There were individual carrot-and-stick consequences for meeting and not meeting the goals.

Once you have decided on what and how you will measure progress, you must, indeed, review those measurements to ensure you and your team are on course to achieving your objective. It's like setting a course with your navigation app on your phone and checking in periodically to see how far you progressed so you can make necessary course adjustments.

Whenever I ask someone the status of a project and hear, "Don't worry about it," I worry about it. This has proven true so many times that it informs a key tenet of management: *ensure*. As managers, we need to ensure things happen. We need to ensure what people say "is done" is actually done.

When I was on active duty as a noncommissioned officer (NCO), we worked with officers who dreaded working for Colonel Krantz. In this colonel's office, on the wall was a poster that read, "Hope is Not a Method." That would pretty much suck the wind out of any statements like, "Well, sir, we've done that, and hopefully, it will be taken care of." Young officers learned quickly never to use "hope" in a sentence around the colonel. "Hope is not a method," he'd state. "How do I *know* that it is taken care of?" In other words, what precisely was to be done?

When assigning tasks, ask the pointed question of the individual, "Will you take responsibility to ensure this is done by this designated time?" Define the parameters of the authority and resources the individual has available to get the job done. Let them know they have oversight of and authority over the project, and they will be held accountable. Then, get the hell out of their way and let them do their job. But be present and available and ask pointed questions during progress meetings.

In the autumn of one year, I took over a Barnes & Noble bookstore. Two experienced assistant managers were running it before I took the helm. They then stepped back into their original roles, and by mid-October, holiday hiring should have been completed and a firm date for training established. I asked the operations manager about the status, and since she had already gone through a holiday season at the store, when she said, "It's all set," I trusted that it was all set. As sales picked up, and the new employees were not yet present, I got concerned. Again, she said, "Don't worry about it, we've got these interviews and so and so will be here."

Okay, I thought, *on to other battles.*

In short, the operations manager did not hire the usual 25 percent overlay to accommodate the holiday rush, and we paid the price for low staffing with less than satisfactory customer service and sales. I later found out she was attempting to keep within a real-time payroll budget—that is, week to week—instead of strategizing the year-to-date numbers to cover in December. Normally, you would take week-to-week sales and plan the following week. In the holiday season, that formula doesn't compute as sales rise exponentially, so you must schedule more people during those times knowing those sales increase as they have every year in the history of the business. The assistant manager wasn't going to pull the trigger until she saw the jump because she was under pressure to maintain budget. My mistake was I didn't trust my gut; I didn't follow up or jump in and accomplish it. I delegated authority to the assistant manager, but the responsibility was mine. Essentially, I blew it and had to answer for the shoddy coverage as evidenced by impatient customers waiting in long lines, or piles of merchandise abandoned by customers who decided the line length wasn't worth the purchase.

I should have asked the assistant early on, "How do I *know* this? Can you show me the schedule you have written? How do I *know* we have enough coverage?" And then I should have double-checked it all. From that point on, I utilized the "trust but verify" methodology. This would have given me time to course-correct and ensure we had enough staff to provide the fast cashiering that customers expect. An unwritten rule in retail is that customers will spend as much time as they want shopping, but when they are ready to go, they're ready to go. Asking early would have also set the tone with the team that this was my expectation of them.

The moral to this morsel: Ask the tough questions, double-check the answer, and trust but verify. As leaders, we must work through other people to get something done. We must delegate but not abdicate.

CHAPTER SIX

COMPOSURE: KEEPING YOUR COOL

As leaders, we lead through the Great Whatever—whatever comes our way and disrupts our perfectly planned strategy for the day. Inevitably, shit happens. Too often, when confronted with a crisis, leaders new in a position will revert to their most comfortable role, which is usually something beneath their position. It's the "Little Me" comfort zone because it is a safe known, versus the scary unknown resulting in growth. It's essential to prevent this creeping effect as it creates a vacuum, because if you are doing a lesser role, who is doing your assigned role? In these circumstances, ask yourself, "What can I do here that no one else can do? What am I paid to do here in my role at this moment?"

It reminds me of Rudyard Kipling's poem "If." The premise of this Victorian-era stoic poem is self-trust and the discipline to keep your head about you amid chaos. I reread this touchstone often, and it is so accurate—so powerful—that I am sharing it here:

If you can keep your head when all about you
Are losing theirs and blaming it on you,
If you can trust yourself when all men doubt you,
But make allowance for their doubting too;
If you can wait and not be tired by waiting,
Or being lied about, don't deal in lies,
Or being hated, don't give way to hating,
And yet don't look too good, nor talk too wise:

If you can dream—and not make dreams your master;
If you can think—and not make thoughts your aim;
If you can meet with Triumph and Disaster
And treat those two impostors just the same;
If you can bear to hear the truth you've spoken
Twisted by knaves to make a trap for fools,
Or watch the things you gave your life to, broken,
And stoop and build 'em up with worn-out tools:

If you can make one heap of all your winnings
And risk it on one turn of pitch-and-toss,
And lose, and start again at your beginnings
And never breathe a word about your loss;
If you can force your heart and nerve and sinew
To serve your turn long after they are gone,
And so hold on when there is nothing in you
Except the Will which says to them: 'Hold on!'

If you can talk with crowds and keep your virtue,
Or walk with Kings—nor lose the common touch,
If neither foes nor loving friends can hurt you,

If all men count with you, but none too much;
If you can fill the unforgiving minute
With sixty seconds' worth of distance run,
Yours is the Earth and everything that's in it,
And—which is more—you'll be a Man, my son!

Source: *A Choice of Kipling's Verse* (1943)

This poem came to mind as I read Charles Duhigg's book *Smarter, Faster, Better*. In a chapter titled "Focus," Duhigg juxtaposes the stories of Air France Flight 447, which crashed into the ocean in 2009, killing all aboard, with that of Qantas Airbus 32 in trouble two years later. The crews responded differently to a similar crisis. In both situations, the crews, bombarded with information, alarms, and blinking lights, signaling system failure after system failure, were drawn into the cognitive tunnel of paralysis. In the latter case, Captain Richard Champion de Crespigny, an experienced pilot, takes over. "Forget about the pumps, forget the other eight tanks, forget the total fuel quantity gauge. We need to stop focusing on what's wrong and start paying attention to what's still working." With that reframing, the crew began ticking off things that were still working. And with that parsed-down information, and the captain keeping his head, they were able to pilot the massive plane safely to the ground. [9]

There have been many times when I have been in situations where others panicked because customers or gangs were threatening the staff, fire alarms were going off, or water main breaks were flooding the store. During those times, and depending on the situation, I take a breath and ask, "What's really going on here? What are the

---

9 Charles Duhigg, "Focus," in Smarter, Faster, Better: The Transformative Power of Real Productivity (New York City: Penguin Random House, 2016), 71.

rules of engagement? What do they want? What do I need to make happen to get what I want?" This framing has helped me de-escalate potentially hostile situations to a more civil outcome or deploy people with actions to solve the problem at hand. "So, catch me up on the problem," or "There are several options here; let's see which one works for you," or "I hear you saying that this happened. I'd be frustrated, too, if that happened to me," or "Call 9-1-1."

I take inspiration from Ernest Shackleton, who led his aptly named Endurance crew through two years of being ice-bound in Antarctica in 1914. Through this time, he kept his crew busy. He maintained composure and, through his leadership, kept his crew motivated, engaged, and … alive. Composure begets composure.

When I was learning to skydive at a civilian school, Accelerated Free Fall, my coach was not feeling well, so he decided to guide me from the ground instead of jumping with me. There was a one-way speaker whereby I could hear him, but he could not listen to me. As my group jumped from the plane at two miles up, it wasn't easy for the ground coach to identify an exiting jumper. Usually, a ground coach would retain what color jumpsuit and shoes the jumper was wearing to spot with binoculars and guide the jumper effectively. Now, I had gone through extensive training and already had a few jumps under my belt. So after my freefall and successful chute deployment at five thousand five hundred feet, I heard him say over the radio, "Turn one-eighty and hold." This command was odd because I would be facing away from the landing zone when the protocol is to face it. I obeyed and continued my eight-hundred-foot-per-minute descent under an open canopy.

So I did my assessment: "What's really going on here?"

I knew there was a runway between me and the landing zone at the airport, and looking over my shoulder, I saw a Cessna at the end, preparing to take off. I looked at the altimeter on my wrist and saw I was now at one thousand two hundred feet. I knew the rule was not to cross the runway below one thousand feet, so at this point, I disregarded my coach, remembering another rule: "Your jump is your responsibility."

I rotated toward the landing zone and charted my flight path, listening to my coach give opposite directions. At this point, I *knew* he was tracking and guiding a jumper other than me. I followed my training, eking over the runway at one thousand fifty feet and making my circle pattern back to the landing zone, narrowly avoiding the runway as I crash-landed downwind. The last thing on the radio was my coach realizing his error, saying, "Oh, shit." I was sore and a tad miffed at the situation, but I was also proud of myself for taking over the jump.

Self-discipline is critical, and a discipline fortified with preparation is gold. There is an unspoken rule in business that those who have the detailed notes or plan wins. Hope is not a method. The detailed plan is the method, its evolution and execution. As Dwight D. Eisenhower famously said, "Plans are worthless, but planning is everything'."[10]

" It's hard, when you're up to your armpits in alligators, to remember you came here to drain the swamp. "

–RONALD REAGAN

---

10 This was his remark at the National Defense Executive Reserve Conference on November 14, 1957, as cited from Dwight D. Eisenhower Presidential Library.

If you're stuck in planning for a great outcome, plan for a poor outcome. Use inverted planning. Inverted planning is imagining the worst outcome, deconstructing how you achieve that outcome, then not doing it that way. It's like that old joke where the patient says to the doctor, "Hey, Doc, it hurts when I do this."

Then the doctor replies, "Well, then don't do that."

Also, the worst result imaginable isn't that bad. If the story doesn't end with a giant asteroid crashing into the earth, then you're probably on good ground. Or, to put it in parachutist parlance, any jump you can walk away from is a good jump.

Chapter Seven

HUMAN CAPITAL MANAGEMENT

The irony of "soft skills" is that they're often the hardest to master. ... Behavioral, social, and emotional skills are what make humans indispensable.

—Adam Grant

Human Capital Management (HCM) is a discipline that used to be called "Human Resources" until someone wisely sussed out that resources are limited and exploitable, and "capital" is an asset. Leadership is a people thing. What were once considered warm and fuzzy "soft skills" are now "hard skills" and very much in demand. But these skills are not hard once you understand that people are people regardless of sex, race, socioeconomic, or academic pedigree. As anthropologist Desmond Morris wrote in *The Naked Ape*, explaining human behavior in the context of the high-tech world, "Even a space ape must urinate."[11] His point is that we are fundamentally made of the same stardust.

We know we need to hire staff to maintain and grow the business. People are people, but they are not fungible. We need the proper person for the role. We need to align values, skills, and "fit"— Can my coworkers and I work with this person?—that will inform our corporate culture. So how do we acquire human capital? We determine which roles we need to fill and post the positions on job boards. Applicants respond, and you interview them to align their skills, strengths, and values with the diverse, vibrant, and productive culture you are trying to create. An HR director once told me, "Sure, you can train a turtle to climb a tree, but wouldn't you rather train a squirrel?"[12] If you are not having success with the applicant pool, recruit.

I have hired hundreds of people in my career, and while I have recruited fewer than twenty, they were the most suitable twenty. If you interview candidates with the mindset of filling the position with the right person who will complement the team, and you know what that looks like, you'll encounter them. It's like the phenomenon of looking for yellow Volkswagens. Suddenly, you see them everywhere. Some like to believe the universe conspires to fill your needs, that your brain is tuned in and hyper-aware, or that you put it out to your network, trusting someone knows somebody who's perfect for the role. Wherever you are on the cosmic, neural, or network continuum, you'll find what you seek.

I was once in dire need of a receiving manager. We posted the position and received many applicants, but I needed someone with

---

11 Desmond Morris, The Naked Ape: A Zoologist's Study of the Human Animal (New York City: Delta, 1999), 23.

12 I think he was paraphrasing Albert Einstein's "If you judge a fish by its ability to climb a tree, it will live its whole life believing it is stupid."

that *je ne sais quoi*, that certain "I know not what," but I'll know it when I see it. After being invited to an associate's house for a cookout, I was introduced to the host's husband Patrick Delaney, who worked in a warehouse, and we struck up a conversation. Throughout the evening, he explained his frustration working in a warehouse, and I kept asking questions. Finally, I told him to give me an example of the workflow of one item flowing through his facility. He chose a well-known brand of microwavable sandwiches and then described each step in the process from when a box of frozen sandwiches entered the building to when it left. He was so thorough that I knew he would be suitable for my available position because he possessed the attention to detail lacking in that department. A few days later, I offered him the job, and he accepted the role. Thanks to the situation—and, I guess, frozen sandwiches—the result was a win-win. Patrick went on to excel at our company, introducing new processes, which made our location one of the most efficient in the company.

Financial planners like to recommend a diversified portfolio—a mix of funds to minimize risks and maximize collective growth. Similarly, we want a mix in our human capital. Both achieve balance: In the former, it allows for ups and downs in markets; in the latter, it allows for diversity of race, religion, gender identification, strengths, and values and creates an ecosystem and a culture that reflect the communities we serve. For example, when I was a young store manager, I enjoyed success in the Holyoke Barnes & Noble. The business was booming, and employees were happy, well-educated experts on the subject matter in their fields, providing excellent customer service. And with over half of the employees being LGBTQ, I thought we were diverse. We hired booklovers. We hired our customers.

I was soon to learn *that* was the problem.

I have had many life-changing and humbling experiences, but one I will never forget is when I was politely summoned to meet with a pleasant gentleman who had been frequenting our café. He introduced himself as Shenandoah Titus.[13]

Shenandoah Titus

"You know, Thom," he said, "I come to your store four or five times a week to work and enjoy your café. But I know when I come in here, I am greeted by a white person, and when I get my beverage from the café, it is served to me by a white person, and when I need a book looked up at the information desk, a white person does that for me and takes me to the section where the book is found. When I check out, a white person processes the transaction. So, I wonder, how do you do your hiring?"

"We typically hire our customers," I replied.

"That's the problem," he said. "As a person of color, I may have all the qualifications you need, but if I am not comfortable being a

---

13 Shenandoah Titus, ESQ, was the Human Rights Director for nearby town Amherst, MA, when he frequented my store. He later became the Founder and Chief Counsel of WARN: Whistleblower Anti-Bullying Resource Network and author of the book, The Whistleblower: Defeating Bullies, Harassers & Management Gang Retaliation.

customer in your store, there wouldn't be the opportunity for me to be hired."

I was floored. He was right. I thought we were doing everything properly, but only 1 percent of our employees were persons of color. Holyoke proper was 47 percent Hispanic. Lesson learned. That one instructive conversation made me redesign our entire hiring model. Opening our channels to a broader array of candidates led to more people of color applying and being hired, which resulted in a much more diverse clientele. Not only was it the right thing to do as a community partner, but it was also the correct business decision.

CHAPTER EIGHT

THE ILM

I love me. I love my life.

Now, I don't always love, or even like, specific circumstances or events, but I view them as quick rain showers on an otherwise sunny day. In general, life is good. I am blessed to have a wonderfully loving best friend who, fortunately, is my wife. I am writing, which is a lifelong dream, and we want nothing that isn't in our control—world events notwithstanding. It's good to count your blessings.

In business, too, counting blessings is vital. It's important to remember all those times you did well, so I keep an "I love me" file, but I title it "ILM" so it doesn't look weird and narcissistic to anyone glancing at my desktop. I got the idea from a commander who had his degrees and certificates all over a single wall in his office called his "I love me" wall. This file is essential because we tend to remember those things that didn't go well. You want to remind your reviewer of the "good things" so they can incorporate it into your positive review.

For example, if you've ever worked in any customer-facing business, and when you get home from work, your significant other asks how your day was, I bet you will start on a story or two about horrible customers. It doesn't matter that the majority of your customers were excellent that day. You talk about the ones who made your blood boil. Knowing this is the human default; it is incumbent upon us as leaders to remind ourselves and those with whom we work that there are more positives than negatives.

Maybe it's human nature. I recall attending a lecture at the University of New Hampshire during the early 1980s where author Stephen King was asked why he writes about all the bad things in life. He said, "The good things take care of themselves." I believe we tend to take good things for granted. But here's where I encourage you not to take them for granted, both for spiritual and monetary reasons—better self-esteem and an increased salary during review.

Scott Adams, the brilliant creator of *Dilbert*, made a comic strip showing the Boss giving Tina her annual performance review. He says he only focused on the past two weeks because he couldn't remember further back than that. However, Tina yells at the Boss, saying she had been on vacation the past two weeks, but the Boss just brushes her off and quickly leaves.[14] I used to show this specific comic strip to my management teams when it came time for reviews. My team needed to write self-assessments to recount their performance the preceding year. It boiled down to what they did to earn the money I paid them the previous year that would have added enough value for me to not only keep them onboard but also justify me paying them more for the upcoming year. It was worded more kindly and concisely than that, but that's what self-assessments are when you get down to it. The management

---

14 "Annual Performance Review," Dilbert Comic Strip, Dilbert by Scott Adams, published January 17, 1997, https://dilbert.com/strip/1997-01-17.

team hated writing these self-assessments because they couldn't "possibly remember" everything they did the previous year, but this was their opportunity to remind me of what they did. It's the halo (good) and horns (bad) effect, and the employee's job is to remind the manager of the halos—I assure you, a manager needs no help in remembering the horns. It was in *their* best interest to make my job easier by being able to justify rate increases.

It is difficult to remember the good things you did last March in February of this year, so that's when your ILM file comes into play. Whether digitally or physically or both, you fill your ILM file with every positive customer compliment, congratulatory corporate email, and benchmark improvements. At the beginning of every fiscal year, I printed out the previous end-of-year metrics and kept a copy in the ILM file for benchmark metrics. Then at the end of the current year, I would pull that out and chart the improvement. Here's why. While in most cases, that data will be provided to you on a current year-over-year data on the latest Profit & Loss (P&L) statement, in my experience, that may not be the whole story you want to tell, so keep all the data you can.

And, count your blessings!

CHAPTER NINE

KNOW YOUR MATHS

In God we trust. All others must bring data.
—DR. W. EDWARDS DEMING

When I started with Barnes & Noble in 1991, the slogan was, "If you paid full price, you didn't get it a Barnes & Noble." It was on television and in the newspapers. In the mid-1990s, the company began positioning itself to go public, enhancing the bottom line. The home office decided to drop the 20 percent off hardcovers and 10 percent off paperbacks to fuel its astronomical growth. There was massive pushback from the booksellers who prophesized losing customers in the bookstore-rich environment—Independents, Borders, Waldenbooks, B. Dalton, and Barnes & Noble being the largest. I had to sell it to my team. Without their support and commitment, the initiative would not likely succeed. It was our job as a profit-generating center for the company to do the company's bidding. It's what we get paid for, and whether we agree with it, we have to support it. So I gathered the supervisors and asked what they thought to air out frustrations, label, and confront their fears. They spit-balled that we would lose 10 percent of our customers.

"For the sake of argument," I said, "let's say we are operating on the standard 40/60 percent discount, where when we buy the book, we pay 60 percent to the vendor, and we keep 40 percent. Let's say the book in question is a paperback, and it retails at $10. The vendor gets $6, and we get $4. We sell that title to ten different customers at the existing 10 percent off for customers. How much profit do we get?

"We'd get $40 to start, but since the book is discounted, we get $30. Ten dollars less 10 percent equals $9 sales price, multiplied by ten customers. The vendor still retains its 60 percent, so it keeps $60.

"Let's move on to the no-discount plan and your scenario where we lose 10 percent of our customers. Now we have nine customers buy the $10 book. We keep $4 and multiply it by nine for each customer, which is $36. The vendor keeps its $60. So we lost 10 percent of our customers, yet we are $6 ahead. (Many customers told me they had not even realized we had discounted books, but I listened to the team's concerns, and then we did the math.)

"Let's lose 20 percent of our customers. That's $4 multiplied by eight customers, which is $32. We are still ahead of the $30."

By this point, they see the bigger picture. *Maybe those guys in the home office really do know what they are doing.* We could withstand losing 25 percent of our customers and be as profitable as with the former discount. And for those customers who run to B. Dalton in the mall across the street, well, most didn't know that Barnes & Noble owned B. Dalton. People tend to think their reality is the *only* reality. The point is: Accept that emotions associated with data points—actual or imagined—exist. Then dissect the problem and engage your team by discovering the answers together.

You win by showing, not by telling.

CHAPTER TEN

MAKING YOUR NUMBERS OR REMEMBER THE MEMBERSHIP!

We will either find a way or make one.
–HANNIBAL BARCA

Memberships and fee-based loyalty cards are cash cows for a company. In Barnes & Noble, they cost $25 and existed as a nontaxable line item on the P&L. A customer would receive a 10 percent discount on their purchases and other special perks. From the company's standpoint, that money was incredible. There was a great deal of pressure on the stores to make at least a 2 percent conversion rate, not only because of the pool of money it produced but also because members shopped more than nonmembers and spent more per transaction—a tremendous upside for the company, but a hard sell to customers. As a store manager, I found this to be a tricky situation; if the booksellers weren't behind it, it wasn't going to happen. This required a change in the bookseller mindset.

Booksellers were, by and large, nerdy, introverted, subject-matter experts. And while the company was built on the backs of introverts, the allure of the free money a membership card afforded was too great to ignore. So what started as a passive program—"Reader's Advantage"—with no quota in the late 1990s, evolved from a 1 percent conversion suggestion to a 2 percent conversion mandate with the name change to "Member". Stores had to hit the numbers, but given the taxonomy of the majority of the workforce, how?

The answer was, is, and shall be: You change the employee or you *change the employee.*

You provide training and encouragement, and then it is up to the employee. Either the employee has the willingness and ability to change their behavior, or they are "promoted to customer"—in other words, terminated—and someone else is brought in to do the job the way you need it done. This is effective, and it moves from the top down. If the employee isn't changed one way or another, the results don't improve, and the supervisor is changed to someone who will change the employee. This process was temporarily successful for the shareholders, but not so much for the other stakeholders. The culture changed from book people who were book finders to membership sellers who also sold books. This changed how we hired associates in a significant way.

My store was struggling with membership conversions, so when Peter Blount, the Regional VP, put his hand on my shoulder and asked me how someone of my ability could allow his store to perform so poorly, I asked him who was the best at it. I wanted to meet this maestro in person. We partnered with my district manager, Beverly Wilson, and I took a road trip to the Bronx to a high-performing store. My operations assistant, Michael Downing, and I made the trip there, and the Bronx manager graciously gave us the spiel you're supposed to say to someone you don't know or trust yet: "Metrics. Leadership Buy-in. This is how we chart everyone's progress." And on and on. But, like anything else in life, relationships matter, and as we got to know each other, he determined we were not a threat. He told us the real turnaround story after I was vulnerable and shared my frustrations about my store.

We had a high-volume music department—keep in mind, this was before the days of streaming and downloading—but the staff couldn't convert customers into members. Their answer was always "All our customers already have a membership and aren't interested." We knew this wasn't the case because we had data showing the conversion rates, which only showed rates of nonmembers purchasing and defined these as "opportunities." In other words, the conversion rate was based on the purchases where a membership was not used, and these were the opportunities to convert to members. I experimented and moved a high-performing salesperson from the main sales area to the music department for a shift and *voilà!*—new memberships increased.

The Bronx manager lit up and shared his actual—albeit, not politically correct—secret to success. When he took over the store, he had experienced a similar problem, with the familiar words "All our customers already have a membership." Even though the data clearly showed that wasn't the case, the booksellers were stuck in their familiar narrative of *can't*. Then arrived the blessing of a personable southern charmer transferring up to New York, and she could sell memberships. As she started tipping the scales at 3 percent, the rest of the staff saw the possibility of success and joined in by upping their charm. So instead of one person carrying the load, the rest of the store bought in and contributed. By changing the personnel, the mindset changed from impossible to possible to probable. It worked. The Bronx manager shrugged it off, saying, "Hey, you've got to find a way to make the numbers."

We all knew it was in our best interests to make the numbers, so we came back, assembled the leadership team, and moved some people around. We hired more people with charismatic personalities and put them up front. So while they weren't necessarily "book people," they were good "people people" and could sell. We had to first change the leadership's mindset on hiring, then execute accordingly. Others who saw what was happening either stepped up or stepped out. I had more than one conversation with a veteran bookseller who ended up saying, "I see where this is going, and I am not interested," and then they resigned. It wasn't easy, but it was necessary to survive as we were, at that time, going head-to-head with Borders and an up-and-comer called Amazon. The result was that Borders went out of business in 2011, and as of now, Barnes & Noble and Amazon—with Prime Memberships—are still going strong.

Sticking with retail for the moment, gift card sales is another area of great importance in the retail world. Gift card-bearing customers tend to frequent the store more often and spend more than the dollar amount on a gift card. But the real profit comes in what is known as "breakage." Breakage is revenue that is recognized from services that are paid for but not used. According to Forbes, the average retail breakage is 2–4 percent.[15] At Barnes & Noble, it was estimated at 7 percent. In the latter example, that's $3.50 off

---

15 Aaron Hurd and Dia Adams, ed., "Breakage Is Worth a Lot of Money," What Is Breakage and Why Does It Matter? (blog), Forbes Advisor, updated June 18, 2021, https://www.forbes.com/advisor/credit-cards/what-is-breakage-and-why-does-it-matter/.

a $50 gift card. That's free money for the retailer, so it's important to know that and embrace why the retailer is fixated on selling gift cards—free money, higher transactions, and more frequent trips to the store. And remember, revenue is recognized when the customer purchases a product or service, not when the gift card is sold.

Retailers must teach people to sell. Selling loyalty cards and gift cards can be tougher than lips on a woodpecker, but perseverance will prevail. Every rejection is one spot closer to closing. The company wins, and you, as a leader, influence that victory.

Chapter Eleven

IN GOOD COMPANY

A t one of the companies I worked for, the management team—this included me—would take their lunches at separate times, sitting at their desks in front of computers while the staff ate their meals in the breakroom. Recognizing this practice as a liability, the company mandated that managers eat their lunches off-site or with the employees in the breakroom. I viewed this dining-together policy as a good move. It was how we used to do it at a Barnes & Noble I managed and bridged the "Us vs. Them" gap wonderfully. It celebrated humanity, not the role. *Hey, look, that manager is just a guy like us, after all.* Plus, the manager would gain a personal understanding of an employee's *why* through casual lunch conversation. The word "company" originates from the Latin *com panis*—*com* meaning "together," and *panis* meaning "bread."

"It originally described how merchants would gather, share stories, eat together, and trade," said David Spinks, author of *The Business of Belonging.* "Companies are communities." [16]

16 David Spinks, The Business of Belonging: How to Make Community Your
   Competitive Advantage (Hoboken: Wiley, 2021).

It is essential to break bread together. In the tight-knit missions I was involved in during my military years, we enjoyed this aspect of the community. We accomplished tasks for *each other*, not for the higher good, whose need was addressed by completing the mission. It is important to note that there is a fine line between this behavior and fraternization. We all knew where the boundary lines were drawn. So, too, in the civilian sector. I've had to terminate a few friends in my time, and, mostly, we remained friends afterward. It's the Ralph and Sam phenomenon from the old Warner Brothers' *Looney Toons* cartoons where Ralph Sheepdog and Sam Wolf punched in a time clock at the beginning of their shift, fought all day, and punched out at night. It was a job. They understood their roles at "work" and presumably enjoyed an amicable relationship outside of work.

While we are on this subject, let's talk about the subtleties to avoid. I cringe when I see signs in a breakroom or office hallway with a directive signed, "The Management." I don't know where this cowardly practice originated, but it needs to stop. If you need to be directive with something better communicated by a sign than face-to-face or email, then have the guts to put your name to it. Don't widen the "Us vs. Them" chasm by being anonymous and hiding behind a fictitious cabal.

The establishment of boundaries, the evolution and adoption of norms around these interactions, allow for a more congenial and enjoyable workplace. This leads to a safer work environment where people take risks and speak up where they may otherwise not. The whole expands as the hole shrinks.

THE ESSAYS

MENTORS AND COMPOSURE

It was 4:30 in the morning in a jungle encampment in Honduras, when I met my commander and mentor, Major Walter H. Debany, at the Army mess tent and grabbed a paper cup of coffee. As was part of our daily ritual every morning before the duty day began, we met and walked around the dirt trail perimeter of the camp and discussed life, the universe, and everything going on in the pre-9/11 world. It was 1999, and the only thing on the worry horizon was the infamous Millenium Bug Y2K and the fear that the computers turning from 1999 to 2000 would wreak havoc because computer dates were two digits.

I was fortunate to have a few good mentors in my life. Walt Debany has since retired at the rank of Lieutenant Colonel to a Civil War-era farmhouse in Gettysburg, Pennsylvania. Those who didn't try to mold me in their image would guide me to find strength in mine. Walt—I'll call him that now that we are both retired from the military—would talk about relationships, finances, the military, and his love for all things Civil War. He is a historian and was fortunate enough to marry another Civil War historian. Those walks meant a great deal to me, and through them, I found inspiration to continue my military career and have success in my civilian life. One of the greatest gifts he gave me was modeling an incredible attitude. When things didn't go right, he would say something like "Yes! An opportunity to make it better!" or "Shit hit the fan, an opportunity to excel!" I've adopted these expressions—this learned optimism— for use in my life. I remember one time when I was the only closing manager, and the opening manager told me several key members had called out for the night, so I would be closing with a skeleton crew—the bare minimum to operate the building. Knowing my team was in earshot and listening for my reaction, I invoked Debany and said, "Excellent! This is our opportunity to shine. All we have to do is keep this afloat for eight hours, and this is the team that can do it!"

Another mentor of mine, Paul Perch, started me on a behavioral science path, which you'll see referenced throughout this book, beginning with Desmond Morris's work *The Naked Ape*. Paul has a nonfiction view of the world and calls things as he sees them. In one heated exchange he and I had outside a building, I subconsciously moved around and stopped this dance on an uneven part of the sidewalk. He interrupted my rhetoric by saying, "You can be taller than me if you want." It took me off guard until he pointed to where I was standing. I was indeed higher than him. Which, again, suggests back to us being, and behaving as, primates at the core. Situations and discussions like this launched me into a deeper understanding of human nature, which helped me become a better leader. They taught me to see things beyond how they present themselves on the surface. An irate customer or a frustrated employee is usually responding to more inputs than the given problem at hand. Understanding the primal and psychological implications helps defuse and solve problems.

I remember another time Paul helped me see this. One day, he and I were walking a retail building to ensure its business-readiness. As we walked by and greeted Cathy, a supervisor of a small department, Paul whispered to me out of her earshot, "See how Cathy is today? When her hair is frizzy like that,—be careful around her. She's having a bad day." On the outside, this may sound like a presumptuous, even sexist, comment to make about someone. Still, we had known Cathy a long time and observed her behavioral patterns. The fact that her hair was frizzy might only mean a late and hurried start, but this would be a rarity. Paul was right, she was on edge that day, but knowing this in advance allowed us to frame our conversations with her and keep her on non-customer-centric tasks to reduce the risk of a bad customer experience.

Paying attention to people daily enables us to discern patterns that allow us to operate more effectively, see what the whole picture is or could be, and then factor those into the issue(s) at hand. The Cathy example could have easily been a disheveled Ken, who normally comes into work with a pressed shirt and clean-shaven. If he comes in wearing a wrinkly shirt and with beard stubble, be aware and be concerned. "How are you doing today, Ken?" is a good opportunity to check on his well-being.

This harkens back to my military days—being taught, then teaching, the importance of inspecting troops in morning formation. To the casual observer, we are standing in front of each soldier and assessing them, looking to gauge their pride reflected in neat and primness of their uniforms. But we are also looking in their eyes. We want to assess their physical and emotional readiness for the day ahead.

Major Dwight Kranz was my unit commander during a challenging point in my personal life, deployed and away from family. Every soldier in the unit was separated from the people they loved, and while we performed our mission, Dwight recognized the person behind the soldier. He took the time to bridge the gap between role and person and genuinely cared for the soldiers serving in his command. One time, he had us all read John Gray's classic *Men Are from Mars, Women Are from Venus*. Because his wife had suggested he read it to understand better how men and women approach situations differently. And, if *he* had to read it, *we* had to read it. I took its lessons to heart, incorporating them into my leadership cache. In a nutshell, men want to fix things, whereas women sometimes just want to be heard.[17] So, my takeaway as a male was, "Shut up and listen." This one lesson informed my personal and business relationships and has served me well. Kranz and his cohort, First Sergeant Caesar Meledandri, both Vietnam combat veterans, provided counsel as much as command and ensured we accomplished our mission as a unit. It was more than a job. This band of brothers mentality stayed with me throughout my military and civilian careers.

Through another commander, Maj. David Durling, I learned perspective. I was First Sergeant at the time, which is the liaison role between officers and enlisted. We discussed how the soldiers were reacting to an Adjutant General (AG) investigation into processes in the units. Durling said, "First of all, soldiers bitch. About everything. Second, if the AG finds something we shouldn't be doing, he'll say, 'That. Don't do that.' And as long as we change how we do it, then we'll be fine." I frequently remind myself of this when dealing with complaints. Listen, apologize, if necessary, fix what's wrong, and move on.

These experiences provided a foundation of composure which I have sought to nurture in my life and leadership.

---

17 John Gray, Men Are from Mars, Women Are from Venus: The Classic Guide to Understanding the Opposite Sex (New York City: HarperCollins Publishers, 1992).

STONE SOUPIN' IT:
THE WISDOM IN
CHILDREN'S BOOKS

In the early day of Barnes & Noble Superstores, we were hiring and opening stores rapidly. Store openings are a fantastic experience where the whole team works together and bonds during the setup well before a customer enters the building. During the morning meetings, a children's book was often read aloud to the team. This gave the future story-time host an audience and brought the group, presumably once children themselves, to a safe space of shared memories. I find a lot of children's literature can be helpful in an adult context. Consider *Harold and the Purple Crayon*. In this Crockett Johnson tale, Harold must solve the problems he encounters. What is often overlooked, however, is that Harold created his problems.[18] It is worthy of a thought-provoking discussion.

Harold aside, my all-time favorite in the business realm is the classic tale *Stone Soup*. Many authors and illustrators have many

---

18 Crockett Johnson, Harold and the Purple Crayon (New York City: HarperCollins Publishers, 1983).

versions out there, but the central premise remains the same. A hungry stranger comes into a famine-stricken town proclaiming to have a stone that makes soup. All he needs to make it work is a kettle of boiling water. The townspeople are skeptical, but our charismatic lead gets them involved by saying, "This is good, but it would be better with cabbage." Once added, he says, "This is much better but would be even better with carrots." And on it goes with each villager contributing some part of their stash until a big, nourishing pot of soup results, which is shared with the village.[19]

So, when I "stone soup it," that's the gist. A leader can bring about change by encouraging everyone's contribution into the pot. The leader's job is to achieve buy-in and then collaboration. If done well, everyone enjoys the spoils. Abraham Lincoln did this by assembling the most competent people in his cabinet. They didn't agree on everything, but this team of rivals accomplished emancipating slaves, winning the Civil War, and keeping the United States intact.

My "stone soup" approach to leadership is the same. I value the often-disparate inputs of a diverse management team, with each offering their contributions of experience, leading to a successful outcome: More cabbage for all. What it boils down to is that most "complex" problems can be solved by parsing down to the simplest parts and getting everyone to contribute. The ideal is consensus, but when that doesn't happen, and the leader makes the decision, at least all have had their say. It's as simple as a children's story.

There's a caveat, though. Stone soup can also be used manipulatively, so you need to be aware of this. For example, you know those ads for nutritional supplements for improved clarity, sex life, or bowel movements? I do and would love for them all

---

19 Marcia Brown, Stone Soup (New York City: Aladdin, 1997).

to be improved by one magic pill. The thing is, you need to be a critical thinker about this. One ad I read recently was for one bottle of ninety capsules. A three-month supply for fifty-four dollars? Nope. Fifteen-day supply breaks down to two tablets, three times a day, each with eight ounces of water. Ironically, the water is the stone in this soup. Consider if you're not a water-drinker and are now consuming twenty-four ounces of water a day, then, of course, you're going to feel better. You'd feel better with just the water. Keep in mind the Latin phrase *post hoc, ergo proctor hoc*, which means, "After it, therefore because of it."[20] In this case, it's a fallacy. You feel better after you take the capsules for a week mostly of your body's gratitude for giving it more water. Water is the primary catalyst for your transformation.

---

20 Not from my extensive knowledge of Latin, but rather from Season 1: Episode 2 of *The West Wing*.

TRAIN(ING) DERAILED

S o, you've hired or inherited a team. Now you must build it, make it cohesive, and better serve the company's goals. That's where Learning & Development come into play.

Competencies, culture, and commitment make a great team. You, as a leader, will be charged with ensuring your team is trained and has the technical competency bolstered by a supportive culture. Competencies require background training and hands-on reinforcement before the individual is expected to perform—crawl, walk, run, as the saying goes. You don't send untrained soldiers into combat, and you do not send untrained personnel into the office or sales floor without giving them the knowledge and tools to do their job.

A typical scenario in high-turnover retail operations has the new employee scheduled in the training room for a week. Meanwhile, some scheduled staff call in sick, compromising your ability to operate the business. What do you do as a leader? Do you stick to the planned training for this person? Are you disciplined enough to have that person stay in the training room while customers and the staff that did show complain about the operation being short-handed? I know the textbook's answer is to bite the bullet and train, but it's a tough call when you're in that position. I've done it both ways, and when I have sacrificed the training for short-term success, I always intended to have that individual go back to training once the crisis is averted. However, there is never a shortage of crises, that good intention is seldom realized, and an untrained employee becomes frustrated, emotionally shuts down, and leaves.

Many companies struggle with this training paradox. Businesses have Learning & Development teams design training platforms and roll them out to business units or retail stores. At the store, the need for bodies on the floor supersedes the perceived necessity of training. As the saying goes, "It's hard, when you're up to your armpits in alligators, to remember you came here to drain the swamp." Put another way, the immediate danger—tasks, customer service, etc.—outweighs the long-term goal: a well-trained staff. For store managers who are held accountable for sales plan on a short-term basis—weekly, monthly, and quarterly—training often defaults to a nice-to-do, not a need-to-do. This is, indeed, a short-sighted approach but is a reality with which to be reckoned. Customers at the door require warm bodies on the sales floor to take care of them.

I have found it best to educate individuals offsite in another building with no expectation for the individual on the sales floor. It's out of sight, out of mind. A little more expensive, to be sure, but the Return on Investment (ROI) is worth it. As a training manager, I would often partner with nearby stores to send a manager over for half a day to run my building while taking my team offsite. We would then reciprocate, and it was a successful approach as it would allow uninterrupted time to focus on team building. I'm a fan of Patrick Lencioni's *Five Dysfunctions of a Team*, and I have been fortunate to lead many iterations of it. The secret sauce is getting enough sequestered time so the team can become vulnerable, which builds trust and understanding among the teammates. After these meetings, the managers would feel more comfortable going to each other to resolve conflicts rather than letting them fester. Going offsite was the best way to accomplish this trust-building endeavor.

Once training was complete, it was necessary to put that person in a position to apply it lest it is forgotten. You've probably seen this while attending conferences or seminars where everyone gets fired up and motivated, then leaves only to return to home base and be sucked back into the routine. One way to overcome that is aggregated wins—little victories that build upon another. Learn and apply. Learn and apply. Then through repetition and success, the skill becomes a habit. Proper staffing is crucial, and when it works, it's a beautiful flow.

There's a business adage that has the Chief Financial Officer (CFO) ask, "What if we train them and they leave?" to which the Chief Executive Officer replies, "What if we don't and they stay?" Building competencies is an essential investment of time and energy to build talent.

THE FOURTH LLAMA: SPIT HAPPENS

At my company, 3 Llama Education, LLC, we were often asked, "Why llamas and why three?" It all started with a decision that was fast-moving from start to finish; idea to execution, a jocular answer to the question "What kind of pet should we get?" Answer: "Llamas." Then to the reality months later of building a paddock, barn, and fence, and finally adding the llamas. My then-wife, Kelli, and I started the farm with three animals because llamas are herd animals, and you can't have just one. They go mad if alone, and if you have two, well, they're just pets. Three was the magic number to establish a herd. The llamas are happiest in that small number as they can vie for which is the alpha, and once that's decided, figure out their respective order in the herd and go about their business of being llamas.

On our farm, Haystack Llamas, we had three purebred llamas named Cody, Morgan, and George. They got along famously after Morgan asserted himself and earned the alpha slot, but we were naïve when another llama farm called and asked if we wanted a fourth llama for free. Llamas can be expensive, and the thought of getting one for free was too appealing. "When you visited us, he seemed to like you," the owner said. "So we wanted to give him to you as a thank you for purchasing the other three boys." So, Stitch moved into the paddock as the fourth llama.

Stitch was considerably smaller in stature than the other three, but that didn't stop him from being the most obstinate and disruptive one in the herd, refusing to fall into order. Morgan tried to put him into place, and by that, I mean *kill* him. Most people think llamas are cute and spit. While both of those are true, llamas are also pretty badass and violent, making them fantastic guard animals. We had to restrain Morgan, which only worked temporarily. Eventually, to prevent him from going berserk, we had to relinquish Stitch back to the previous owner's farm. Sadly, the herd was never the same.

Why does this matter? A lousy acquisition can *Yoko Ono* a well-functioning team.[21] So, vet and choose wisely, set clear expectations, and establish norms—which are agreed-upon standards of conduct. Manage performance until all cylinders are firing together—leadership is not "Set it and forget it." Do not hesitate to remove the offender if performance improvement actions are ineffective.

In the case of the llamas, removing Stitch was the solution, but it was too late. The fourth llama ruined a good thing. Ironically, adding a Stitch unraveled the herd.

---

21 Many fans credit John Lennon's girlfriend, Yoko Ono, as responsible for breaking up the Beatles in 1970.

GETTING TO THE
GOTTA-GET-TOS

My wife, Sharon, and I like jigsaw puzzles. We like the journey of finding pieces and their interlocking partners out of the chaos of a mound of cut cardboard, creating a beautiful image. Often, these images are thought-provoking and engender lovely conversations. We did a puzzle one recent Saturday night with a collection of book covers, which prompted many have-you-read-this discussions. It took us hours to finish because there were so many pieces and we kept distracting each other talking about books we've both read. Seated across from one another at the kitchen table, we sipped wine and listened to streaming smooth jazz as we worked. It was a lovely experience.

The thing was, we had that puzzle for about two weeks. It was a thoughtful housewarming gift, and it was appropriate because we are both word nerds and love books. But the puzzle, with all its potential energy stored in a box, sat in plain view for that time. It was right in front of us, but so was the myriad of other distractions and gotta-get-tos in our lives. One morning, as I sat with my coffee, listening to an audiobook on life design, I grabbed the box, unsealed it, and began placing the pieces on the table. What prompted the action, I do not know. I just started looking for the flat-edged side pieces, as if hunting for the peanuts in a box of Cracker Jacks like when I was a kid. I gathered as many of the side pieces as I could find and put some together before I had to stop to take care of the business of life, leaving the very unfinished puzzle on the table. A couple of days later, Sharon came home, saw the puzzle, and teasingly said, "Ah, you started without me." But, seeing the potential energy released, we set forth on its completion.

"When you pray, move your feet."

—African Proverb

It occurs to me that, many times, life is like that. We buy a book, only to have it live its life unread on the shelf. We dream a dream, only to let it wither on its gotta-get-to branch. We like the idea of something more than we like the work that needs to be put into it. That is, until it gets started and the potential energy is released. And then, it's game on. Whether it is writing the first sentence in the novel we want to publish or tying the shoelaces on the running shoe that will carry you out the door on a cold morning when you want to stay in bed, it's about getting past the idea of wanting to do something, wanting to be something, and then doing it. That's all it takes. In your personal life or as a leader, it's important to jump in and get the project going. Action precedes outcome.

Once upon a time, I worked in a bookstore with a great man named Christian House. Christian was a math geek and adored by all who knew him for his quirky sense of humor and honest assessment of things. One day, he and I were standing in front of a very heavy bookcase needing to be relocated. As we puzzled out how to best accomplish this, he turned to me and said, "Thom, all we need to do is overcome the coefficient of inertia." We needed to put it on furniture sliders and budge it from its carpet-indented grip. Once the initial thrust created motion, it wasn't difficult to continue moving the bookshelf. Once we put the work behind the idea, it was mission accomplished.

THE MANY "ME'S"

A friend of mine, when asked what she does, shrugs and says, "I wear many hats." It is the soft precursor to a more in-depth recapitulation of the many ways she helps people. I don't have as many hats. I have "Me's"—as in, many versions of me. There's the one who writes, the one who competes, the one who teaches, and the one who leads people and manages things. All are competent and welcome. I wanted a "Mini-Me,"[22] popularized in the Austin Powers franchise, but that was not to be. Instead, I have a "Little Me." And he's a bastard.

I first encountered this expression while watching Netflix's Jerry Seinfeld's *Comedians in Cars Getting Coffee*. In a café conversation with Seinfeld, Jim Carrey nails this concept of identifying the very human characteristics that sidetrack our higher selves[23]. Jealousy and doubt, for example. Knowing this or just having a way to

22 Mini-Me: (1) A person who resembles a smaller or younger version of another
   person. (2) A person who adopts the opinions or mannerisms of a more powerful
   or senior person to win favor, achieve promotion, etc.
23 *Comedians in Cars Getting Coffee*, season 6, episode 3, "We Love Breathing What
   You're Burning, Baby," directed by Jerry Seinfeld, written by Jerry Seinfeld, featuring
   Jerry Seinfeld and Jim Carrey, aired June 17, 2015, on Netflix, https://www.netflix.
   com/search?q=comedians%20in%20&jbv=80171362.

identify and label it is helpful. For Carrey, it was the "Small Me." I know some cancer patients who anthropomorphize and name their visualized malignant tumor to focus energy to combat it. Naming this emotional malignancy helps similarly.

Little Me is the "Treasonous Saboteur" and must be dealt with as such.

If I perceive a person behaving like someone who has cheated me in the past, Little Me jumps to the conclusion that this person is doing the same thing. However, it might not be the case. Little Me is full of fear and distrust, projecting the mistakes and betrayals of the past onto the promise of the future. This fear creates a self-fulfilling prophecy, where a relationship is compromised not because of something the person did, but because Little Me gaslighted me.

It is beneficial to recognize this threat, then categorize, immobilize, and euthanize it. It begins with the recognition of what you are feeling and then goes from there. It took me many months—I almost sabotaged a new relationship—but once I got a bead on the little bastard, I was able to make him go away. Of course, there are still times when he starts to peak around the corner. Whenever that happens, I flick it away like an encroaching ant. I shared this with my then-girlfriend, who said these words: "Little Me in a man never won a woman's heart."

There are other philosophies out there, such as in Richard Carson's acclaimed classic book, *Taming Your Gremlin*, or in books by Brené' Brown, where you recognize fear and doubt, invite them in, but don't trust them with your jewelry. I'm not as kind, and for me, I squash it. Whichever path you choose, I implore you not to give it power. You have agency and must utilize it to the fullest to take command of your life. And if Little Me is correct in his caution, so be it. Trust me. It will be so, so much better when you do.

But then, there's another Little Me: Mighty Mouse. You know, the "Stand back. I'll protect you! Here I come to save the day!" kind of internal protector. Your Mighty Mouse is your Little Me jumping in to save the day, to protect you from threats imagined. He's your internal operating system kicking in the fight-or-flight response. We all have it, thank God. It's what keeps us from petting bears, I suppose. The thing is, we must manage it. We must lead it. We must recognize its place at the table as an advisor in our cabinet. It's an assistant who offers *a* voice, not *the* voice. So, when you hear it, consider it, thank it, and make your own decision.

The corollary is, it's not just you. The people you're dealing with on a day-to-day basis have Mighty Mice and Little Me's. I don't care how evolved your emotional operating system is, when there's a real or perceived threat, people revert to their Primal Operating System (POS). If you can recognize the POS in yourself and others and label it as such, you can regain composure and get about your business. I touched upon this in the previous chapter on mentors, how you see beyond what is presented as the issue. The "issue" is informed by what that person is experiencing and *has* experienced. For example, an employee becomes upset after being denied a promotion. In this case, that denial may bring up a rejection they received in their personal life, and that becomes a "Little Me" spiral of "No one wants me." To sum it up, things are often not what they seem at the surface. A good leader understands this and can soften the blow with specifics as to why the person did not get the promotion. This can allay their fears and allow them to feel disappointed, not disrespected.

THE THOUGHTY BITS

(HOW) ARE YOU EXPERIENCED?

*All of us are probably three people. We're probably
the person that we think we are, and we're probably
the person that you or somebody else perceives us to be,
and ... frankly, we're probably somewhere in the middle.*

—MICHAEL OVITZ

I n his 1967 album, Jimi Hendrix asks, "Are you experienced?"
The answer is always yes!

You *are* experienced by everyone you meet. What you wear
and how you stand and speak inform how other people experience
you. So you want to influence that experience by understanding it.

In the Army, creating and maintaining "military bearing" through
cadence singing in moving formations instills self-confidence.
"Standin' tall and lookin' good, oughta be in Hollywood" is an
example of this. This motto informs the mindset and manifests in
the individual's comportment, and thus how the soldier feels about
his or herself *and* how others experience them.

In one-on-one meetings, it is informative to ask team members, "How do you think other people experience you?" This question also works when you are interviewing job candidates. Try it, and bonus points if you invoke the Socratic Method and follow up with "And why do you think that is?"

LOYALTY AND COMMITMENT
VS. OBEDIENCE
AND COMPLIANCE

A former District Manager once said to me about the new direction our company was taking: "Well," she said, "this isn't going to sound good, but we don't need your department managers to *think*. We need them to *do*." It was a difficult pill to swallow because I cultivated teams and solicited input on driving business, fostering a collaborative environment.

I had a similar experience at the Fortune 50 company. Here, we found our fundamentals lagging under a tenured crew of associates accustomed to operating in a low-accountability environment. The store manager here was frustrated and switched to a very, shall we kindly say, *directive* approach. The operation looked great. The morale sucked. It got me wondering if this is not the better approach. Is it better, as Machiavelli wrote, to be more feared than loved?

I was faced with the choice of leaving my Stephen Covey-istic "seek first to understand"[24] and adopt a binary approach of it

---

24 Stephen R. Covey, *The 7 Habits of Highly Effective People* (Salt Lake City: FranklinCovey, 2016).

being perfect or it's not—it's either done, or it is not. This was not tough because I'm more of a 100 percent fast, 80 percent right kind of guy, and I would rather have a commitment from the team instead of compliance. I've lived the latter before, where the pay is supposed to be a consolation for the loss of hours and agency. It is not sustainable, and it is not correct. It is a slow bleed, where working under the oppression of time, talent, and treasure constraints drains the energy. Being surrounded by malaise and ennui is contagious and can lead to more of the same. When you are loved and love your team, that reciprocity leads to loyalty you cannot buy. It's a great feeling to have.

It is better to be respected enough that people know that we are all in this together, and those who are not pulling their weight will be held accountable. People want to feel valued. They want to feel they matter.

"The best leaders do not need to sell you," author and consultant Sharon E. Reed says. "They lead quietly, generously, and consistently. By the gift of their own example, they attract and earn a loyal following."[25] Loyal employees are committed to their leadership or to the cause. Obedient employees are committed to self-preservation and compliance. Individuals must choose between the two behaviors: commitment or compliance. The latter is fear-based and results in poor decisions being made (see Chapter Five).

As I said previously, it's about reciprocity. The whole ecosystem functions better when it is holistic and has a "We're all in this together" approach to the team. Because then, *then*, my friend, the Machiavellians would concede it is better to be loved.

---

25 Sharon E. Reed, *Walking the Heart Path: Bite-sized Bits of Wisdom on Living & Leading from the Inside Out* (Davidson: Heart by Design, 2017).

EMBRACE EMPATHY

If having empathy isn't your strong suit, get someone with empathy to do the hiring. Leaders with no empathy tend to hire staff with low empathy. If you want a team to function in a positive workplace and have outstanding customer service and sales, you must embrace empathy. You must overcome the natural bias to hire your likeness. We desire to hire people like ourselves, but everyone is best served when we employ those who complement us, fill in our skill gaps, and reflect the demographics of our community.

How to Lose a Customer

For many reasons, I have bank accounts with different banks. One of them has notoriously bad customer service. In one instance, there was one teller at the window a line of eight patrons deep. An employee was sweeping the floor, and the manager was standing in line with a pad trying to sign people up for a program. The tellers did not look up and acknowledge patrons, and the manager was oblivious to it all—no attempt to call backup, no acknowledgment of the situation.

Another time in the same bank, I had an issue with a deposited check being held for a week in a well-established account. I went to the manager, who was on the other side of the counter, and explained the situation. He prattled on about policy and that I needed to contact them every time I deposited a check with them to ensure it would be cleared. At no point did the manager come around the counter and engage me, preferring to have the wall between us. It was then I made the correlation between the level of the staffing customer service. If the manager did not hire them, he modeled the behavior.

Conversely, another bank always has excellent customer service. I am greeted immediately upon entering, and the tellers are conversant. As a result, I no longer do business with the low-empathy bank.

MANTRAS FOR
MANAGING UP

Everyone works for someone. Sometimes it is necessary to "manage up" to that someone to improve the relationship and the organization. Here is some advice:

1. There's a difference between "agree with" and "support." Your job is to support the boss and company so long as their direction is legal and ethical.

2. Go ugly early. Bad news doesn't get better with age. Don't let your boss be blindsided.

3. Have dignity in all things. Respect the position or role or rank if not the person and counsel in private whenever possible. As my father used to say, "You salute the rank, not the person."

4. Reassure your supervisor that you are in their corner; you know your position and genuinely want them to succeed.

5. Avoid the "loser loop" of petty whining and challenge your coworkers. "Did you mention it to [the manager]?" Issues do not get resolved by complaining in a circle. Get the issue to the level where it can be fixed. Everyone, especially your supervisor, will appreciate it.[26]

26 A former colleague of mine, Karen Lynn, proffered this advice to her employees

BE THE ALCHEMIST

D o you want to know the secrets to transform lead into gold? Here are the secrets to spinning gold star performance:

- Treat people with dignity and respect.
- Listen to them and *hear* what they are saying.
- Show them you care by *actually* caring and taking action to improve an aspect of their work or personal life, making their existence better. It will ultimately make your existence better as well.
- Lead them with an intentional bias to their growth and success, which begets organizational growth and success.
- If you do these things, then you will have transformed the "led" into gold.

NAVIGATING THE
HUMAN TERRAIN

"How can I help you?" These five magic words are the grease to get the gears turning.

One time, I was working for a company experiencing severe supply-chain issues due to the pandemic. Everyone was in the same boat, but my area of responsibility was one of the hardest hit, and there was a finite amount of material being divvied out to the stores in the enterprise. I needed to be moved up on that list, so I sought counsel from my manager, Philip Mancuso. He suggested the magic five-word technique: "How Can I Help You?" I reached out to the buyer, then recognized and labeled the situation. I expressed sympathy for what he must be dealing with, explained my case, and asked, "How can I help you so that we can solve this?"

He said he would look into it and get back to me, which he did. The following week, our supplies were at par. Instead of getting yelled at or disparaged at every turn, the recipient of the magic five words was relieved and grateful for the respite. He showed his appreciation by moving us up on the distribution list.

I believe most people want to do a good job. They want to do the right thing. So, let's help them help us.

THE PETER PRINCIPLE

Laurence J. Peter's premise in his 1969 book *The Peter Principle* is that "every employee tends to rise to his level of incompetence."[27] The skills necessary to get the position are not the skills required to operate effectively in that position. Being a great doctor may not translate into being a great hospital administrator, and an excellent teacher may not be an excellent principal. While there are many examples of successful transitions, the point is the positions require different skill sets.

This is important when considering promoting an excellent salesperson. That person may not be an excellent sales *manager*. It's an easy trap to fall into as a manager eager to fill a role, and you've got a super-strong performer who wants that position but may not have the skill set for that particular role. These are challenging waters to navigate as the individual applying, who wants the increased status and pay, believes they are the best for the position. That may well be, but you as a leader must ensure that person has the desire, knowledge, and ability to fill that specific role.

And if you do decide to promote that person, understand that their development level resets and requires situational leadership.

27 Dr. Laurence J. Peter and Raymond Hull, *The Peter Principle: Why Things Always Go Wrong* (New York City: HarperCollins, 1969).

SITUATIONAL LEADERSHIP

I could talk at length about this most crucial aspect of leadership, but luckily for both of us, I don't have to because there are outstanding books on the subject by the creators of "Situational Leadership," Ken Blanchard and the Center for Leadership Studies.

Here's a common mistake: You have a high performer in one area, then a position comes open, and you believe they can deliver the same level of performance in that position. In one retail operation, a head cashier had been with the company for over ten years. She was excellent at the job and well-liked by customers and employees for her positivity. She nailed the metrics. When a sales floor department supervisor position came open, this person interviewed for it. Leaning on rewarding performance, and, frankly, the perceived easy way out, the manager promoted this person believing it to be a no-brainer given the aforementioned reasons. You probably see where this is going. The individual floundered because the manager treated her as though she were at the same competency level in her new role as in her old role. The individual failed in the new position, and the manager had to start the process all over. The consequence was the manager losing some credibility with her team and this individual feeling defeated.

The manager made a Little Me error, seeking the path of least resistance, relying on emotion and not seeing the whole picture. I cannot stress the importance of Situational Leadership enough. In the Situational Leadership model, the head cashier was performing at a Readiness Level 4 (R4)—high competence and high commitment—so the management's Supportive Behavior (S) was at Level 4 (S4)—low directive and low supportive.[28] When the individual was promoted to department supervisor, she should have been viewed as an R1—low competence but high commitment—as she was excited about the position but didn't have a grasp of it. The manager should have met that with an S1—high directive, low supportive—response instead of expecting the same level of self-direction.

The lesson is that no matter how good the person is, the role is new to them, and we need to set that person up for success.

---

28 "Readiness" is referred to as "Developmental" in early works. A complete overview of Situational Leadership can be found at www.situational.com.

WHAT'S AT STAKE?

D id you see that billboard on the way to work? Did you hear that advertisement on the radio? What about the ads on your social media? These cost money. The company you work for is spending a great deal of cash and brainpower to draw customers into the business to spend their money to pay your salary. This Customer Acquisition Cost (CAC) must be considered when dealing with customers.

I've had to coach numerous employees on this. There are times when the rules must be bent to satisfy the customer in front of you. As managers, we usually have the authority to do what is necessary to satisfy the customer. We want them to return to our store or our website. If they are unhappy, let's do what we can to remain profitable in the long term by making exceptions. Again, the policy for the manager is to protect assets. Reputation is an asset. What's the right thing to do?

Consider the stakeholders, those who are interested in the company and the outcome of its actions.[29] The Corporate Finance Institute defines the following types of stakeholders:

1. Customers—Stake: product and service quality and value
2. Employees—Stake: employment income and safety
3. Investors—Stake: financial returns
4. Suppliers and Vendors—Stake: revenues and safety
5. Communities—Stake: health, safety, economic development
6. Governments—Stake: taxes and GDP

As leaders, we must be aware of all these. We are focusing on customers and employees for this book, and our job is to create an environment where we can acquire them, keep them, and organically increase the amount they spend with us. There's a lot at stake here.

---

29 "What is a Stakeholder?" Stakeholder, Corporate Finance Institute, https://corporatefinanceinstitute.com/resources/knowledge/finance/stakeholder/.

BUT I'M RIGHT!

A new manager has their ego fueled by the promotion. It's the downfall of many who think it is more important to *be* right than to *do* right. As a leader, you must create a safe environment so your team understands that your decisions aren't personal. Finding the right solution—not basing your decisions on whether a person is right or wrong is the path to continued success.

I have interceded in many employee-customer disputes where the employee adhering to the policy was technically correct, but the solution for the customer and the business was *more* correct. You must understand a few things here for context: Customer Acquisition Cost (CAC) and Lifetime Value (LTV). It costs money to get customers into a store—advertising, multi-channel, etc.—and this cost varies by industry. And once in the store, the customer's value to the business extends beyond the initial interaction. In other words, we want to keep the customer coming back and spending more time and money with us, and that is the customer's LTV to the business.

The issues I have encountered most often are when dealing with customer returns. There are a very expensive minority of customers who abuse return policies, and it is those for whom the return policy is written. When an employee argues with a customer that the store has a thirty-day return policy with a receipt, and the customer comes back thirty-five days after purchasing and wants a refund on a seven-dollar item, I say give them the return. Why? Because I know that our CAC is thirty dollars, I am not going to lose a customer over seven dollars. That would be silly. I will add that during this interaction, I help the employee save face by explaining to the customer that the store has this return policy in place, and the employee is following policy. "We are going to honor the return because we value you as a customer and want you to have a great experience so we can see you again."

Later, in private, I then explain to the employee the *why* and *what* of the transaction and my decision, reaffirming and thanking the employee for doing their job and protecting the company's assets. Further, I explain that our reputation is also an asset which has to be protected as well.

It is more important to do the right thing than to be right.

Reputation Is an Asset

By Mike Mooney, reputation expert and author of
Reputation Shift, 5 High Performance Truths for Success

"There's false thinking that a company, itself, builds its reputation. That's impossible. The reality is that the reputation of the company is built upon the shoulders of every person who represents the brand. Therefore, the company's reputation is either strengthened or tarnished with each individual's interaction with customers, colleagues, and other key stakeholders— what is said or unsaid, what is done or not done. Just as employees should be trained on the company's standards and polices, they must also be inspired and motivated to uphold and grow its reputation.

A company's reputation is a tangible asset and a competitive differentiator for leaders focused on customer and employee retention as well as customer and employee acquisition. Perhaps you would agree that those are key business areas for any leader upon which to focus? If so, then recognizing that being right may cause irreparable harm to your company's reputation instead of doing right that would build reputation and increase customer LTV. Building LTV is much like building a reputation—it takes consistency and time! There are no short cuts for that."

YOU CAN'T TALK TO CRAZY

I n retail and hospitality situations, I've found that people coming in to lodge a complaint or to make a return have rehearsed their argument beforehand and are expecting confrontation. This is good to know as it prepares you by giving you an ego-out. You approach the customer calmly and explain the situation. Sometimes, he is missing some documentation that prevents you from satisfying him. What I do here is listen first, and then repeat my understanding of what he is telling me. And if the answer is "no," then it is *no*, but try to find a qualified *yes*. This is, "I hear what you're saying, and what I need to be able to help you is 'X.'" Most times, this defuses the problem. Also, let's try saying "Let's see how we can solve this together." In the film *Jerry Maguire*, there is the iconic line "Help me help you,"[30] which I am not ashamed to admit I've used on more than one occasion. This involves the customer/client in the solution. The customer now has a part in the outcome by having to provide a receipt or another proof of purchase. If the customer is confident you will do your part, they

30 Cameron Crowe, *Jerry Maguire*, directed by Cameron Crowe (Culver City: Sony Pictures Releasing, 1996), 139 min.

are more likely to do theirs—and be part of the solution—so the situation can be resolved.

And sometimes, you can't resolve a situation easily. Sometimes, people are just frustrated, angry, or mentally challenged. In these cases, it's best to remember the adage of a friend of mine, Honey Lapcharon: "You can't talk to crazy." So, please don't bother wasting your intellectual ammo arguing in circles; it is not worth the psychic cost.

DIFFICULT CONVERSATIONS

I am not giving him hell. I am telling him the truth,
and it feels like hell.

—HARRY TRUMAN

People should always know where they stand with you. Simply put, be straight with people. Sometimes, the truth hurts, and people may be angry with you for hurting them, but they'll respect after a while. They'll appreciate the fact you dared to tell them what they are doing is not up to standard, so long as the criticism is constructive. Keep in mind, too, that the criticism is conveyed privately and civilly for a few reasons: 1) It helps people maintain their dignity; 2) there's no place for anger, profanity, or threats because these then become the message instead of the employee's performance; and: 3) everything you say can and will be used against you. Just assume your words will be repeated to coworkers and family members, so be sure to be measured and meaningful.

Sometimes, a written warning is necessary. This is often called a "Performance Improvement Plan" or a "Performance Development Plan." It is essentially a document stating the behavior that needs to be corrected, why it needs to be corrected, and action steps and timeline required to attain the desired behavior. You must schedule a date for follow-up, and your expectations for improvement must be clearly outlined. An example might be "Progress should be immediate and ongoing. If improvement is not made, further disciplinary action will occur, up to and including your termination." Documenting all dates and outcomes covers your *ass*ets and shows the employee you are serious about their performance.

The setting for these meetings should be in an office, and make sure the person being counseled is near the door. I have seen some instances where managers seat the person being counseled on the inside of the office away from the door, effectively blocking their exit. This should never occur. The person being counseled must feel safe. Also, when having these discussions, it is advisable to have a witness in the room. This witness will not participate but is there to provide comfort and cover, thus mitigating the likelihood of accusations of quid pro quo, sexual harassment, or other threats.

Touchbase meetings between supervisors and staff should be scheduled and routine. It's crucial for both parties to do this. One regret I have is that I didn't take this seriously at points in my career. Managers who were doing a good job running things weren't on my list of priorities. Even though I intellectually recognized that these meetings were necessary, the fires that needed to be put out in other areas of my operation warranted my attention more than the good things. In my rationalization, I'd say, "You're fine, doing well, keep doing what you're doing," to postpone the meeting. This course wasn't meeting their needs as people, and I failed a few managers in not giving them their due. The lesson here is to make time for them. They've got your back, so make sure you've got theirs in all areas, not just the problem ones.

"You should have monthly meetings with your managers to see how they're doing," says Malcolm Macdougall, Chief Solutions Engineer at Organizational Performance Group, LLC. "This is the expectation for your position." Macdougall has been leading and coaching people for three decades and knows the importance of setting agreed-upon work tasks and deliverables. He manages the process through coaching conversations.

As he coaches his leaders on leading, he is often struck when they say "That's going to be a tough conversation" when preparing for their meeting with a nonperforming employee.

Macdougall replies, "How tough could it be? Didn't you sit down and lay out what this person was supposed to do and what the deliverables were? This conversation won't be difficult at all. All you have to say is, 'We agreed on them together, so now let's talk about how we are accomplishing them.' As a matter of fact, if you give the person a chance, they're going to tell you what they have or have not done because there's a good idea of what's being measured against."

Malcolm Macdougall

ROLES

It's not enough to know your place. It's essential to understand why you have that role, and why the position exists in the first place. As leaders, we cannot forget to explain to employees why their job exists and how it benefits the whole organization.

I remember speaking with a front-end loader at a well-known home improvement store. In this person's view, all he did was run around during his shift, bringing in shopping carts and lumber carts, and helping customers load products. He felt it was trivial work and a thankless job. We talked it through, and this is how it went:

Me: So, why do you think they're so many carts out here?

Him: Customers leave them there.

Me: Why did they bring them out?

Him: To carry the stuff they buy in the store to their car.

Me: So, I guess carts must be pretty important to the customer and the store.

Him: (pause, thinking) Yeah.

Me: So, if the carts weren't there, they probably either
wouldn't shop here, or they wouldn't buy as much.

Him: (pause, still thinking)

Me: Well, I am glad you are here doing this work because the
store wouldn't function well without you doing what you're
doing. So thank you!

Him: Thanks, man.

INPUTS INFORM OUTPUTS

When I was a lad in Londonderry, New Hampshire, my best friend was Raymond Turner. He lived in a lovely house across the street from me, and we spent a great deal of time being boys in the 'hood. We lived in rural New Hampshire, so it was more like *Robin Hood*. Anyway, Raymond was sure of two things: 1) He was the only person in the world named "Raymond," and 2) the way he had been taught to play the card game "Go Fish" was the *only* way there was to play it.

We've grown apart over the years and lost contact, but I assume he has reconciled those beliefs. I share this point to express how we are informed and programmed certain behaviors that become our realities until something else comes along to change our minds. This comes into play in leadership when recognizing that a person's behavior is a product of inputs, many of which they have had no control over. They repeat what they say. Consider this: After behaving or saying something in a particular way, have you ever said, "Oh my God, I've become my parents!"? We are mimicking learned behavior. Everyone does it.

As leaders, we must consider this conditioning and provide an alternate input to help employees reframe situations. We might say something like "Have you considered ...?"

GET YOUR MBA

If you want to thrive, you must learn. Always be reading and making a better you than you were yesterday. Formal business education is helpful, and a Master of Business Administration is required for some roles. But do you have to be credentialed to be qualified?

"We are all on a learning curve, and we are always on that learning curve every time we get a promotion or a new job," Chief Solutions Engineer Malcolm Macdougall says. He defines MBA as, "*Model* the *Behavior* until you *Acquire* it and surround yourself with people who are demonstrating that behavior. That's how you are going to acquire it."

DO YOU MEAN
TO TELL ME …?

A policy is generally a codification of best practices. Policies can and should change with technological and social advances, but they should change after being adequately vetted, not because you think you know better.

I was all that and a bag of chips when I started managing. Or so I thought. I was an Assistant Store Manager at Barnes & Noble in New Hampshire, then I was promoted to Store Manager of a new store in a nearby town. Along with fifteen of the existing store's staff, I took an Assistant Store Manager and a department supervisor, who I knew was her boyfriend, when I transferred. Being in a relationship with someone who reports to you is against policy for a good reason, but I knew it wouldn't be a problem in this case since I knew everything. I did not disclose their relationship to anyone. Turns out, I didn't know everything, and when problems inevitably arose, my District Manager, Lynne Nybo, was called in to mediate. Her discovery of the relationship resulted in a private chat in my office, during which time she leaned across the desk and said pointedly, "Now, wait a minute, you mean to tell me you knew about this and didn't say anything?" The problem eventually worked itself out, but that early lesson was ingrained in my mind. As the saying goes, "One 'aw shit' wipes out ten 'atta boys.'" Lesson learned.

When someone considers doing something contrary to the current company policy, I tell them the above story. I then ask them, "Do you want to be sitting here across from the District Manager and have her say, 'Do you mean to tell me you knew the policy but decided to break it because you felt it was wrong?'"

Go ugly early. If something is wrong or you feel it needs to be a certain way, take a partner with your supervisor. The story I told above was one of the challenging ones, which informed me to go and make better choices. In taking a partner, I have been able to change policy. That's the key here: work to change the policy and procedure, first. Don't go rogue.

WE DON'T DO IT
THAT WAY HERE

"I know it says to do it that way in the operations manual, but we don't do it that way here."

Sound familiar? I've encountered this countless times, usually by legacy managers. These managers have always done it one way, so they train people that way. When I take over a new operation, the following conversation inevitably occurs:

Employee: They said not to do that.

Me: Who's "they"?

Employee: Well, I don't remember, but some manager came here and said that. We've always done it this way.

Me: Well, how about we do it the way the company says until we hear otherwise?

I call the employee's point of view in the above dialogue "Management by Mythology." This passing down of apocryphal information is a well-intentioned but not well-formed territorial response. As above, always go to the source document. Always ask, "Where does it say that?"

And, if you find that perhaps the employee's way is more beneficial, then work through your chain of command to change the procedure or policy.

A corollary of this is "Everyone is saying ...." In my experience, it's not everyone. It's that person and two friends engaged in an echo chamber of complaining. It's important to call it for what it is, which is this person feels a certain way. To get to the real problem and source, I would ask, "Everyone? We have a staff of one hundred fifty, and you're saying that you and one hundred forty-nine other people feel this way?"

"Well, no, I mean ...."

"What is really happening here? What is frustrating you? How can I help you?" Then you get to the crux of the situation, and once you have that, the employee—and, presumably, one hundred forty-nine other people—feel heard. Bonus points if you can resolve the problem at hand.

RAPID FIRE

- Redoing things. I hate going backward and retracing my steps. If you do not have time to do it right the first time, when will you have time to do it over?
- When you make a mistake, apologize for it once, make amends, correct it, and then move on. As writer Aldous Huxley said in the foreword to *Brave New World*, "Rolling in the muck is not the best way of getting clean."[31]
- Know your capacity and set boundaries. Protect your time. There is a belief that "When you want something done, give it to a busy person." When you're at capacity, it's okay to say no and that you don't have the bandwidth to give it the attention it deserves. Your life will be better once you embrace this.
- Sometimes, you must be directive. Your responsibility is to ensure that the mission is accomplished, and you must assert your authority.

---

31 Aldous Huxley, Brave New World (New York: HarperCollins, 1998).

- A leader is not in that position to make friends. The expectation is that the leader governs with fairness, equity, and respect. You accomplish the mission and take care of your people.
- Leadership is dancing in the gray between the two black rails of "Is it legal?" and "Is it ethical?" So long as you stay within those rails, your decision to accomplish intent is usually safe.
- At the end of the day, it's the end of the day. On particularly rough days, sometimes all you can do is survive and let your team know what's going on and how you all will get through it together. "We've just got to keep this afloat for eight hours. We can do it." Then, get through the wobbly bits and call it a day. With tomorrow's sunrise, there's a new opportunity.
- Be fair and *consistent* with how you treat people. It's the right thing to do. No favorites.
- What are the optics? You must always be aware of how something looks or could be perceived. How will this look?
- Be flexible. Plans, no matter how seemingly solid, need to evolve, to roll with the flow. As boxing legend Mike Tyson said, "Everyone has a plan until they get punched in the face."

PRO TIPS AND THE
GAME CHANGERS

- Focus on strengths. The old school of thought was to identify the weakest performer and seek to raise those. But that is a fallacy. The best chance of winning is to optimize the winners. Make the winners better. If it's inventory, allocate more space to the highest performers and whittle down the nonperformers. Embrace the Pareto Principle, acknowledging 80 percent of your results are coming from 20 percent of your assets.[32] This applies to people, inventory, and investments. Bet on the winners.

- Be the rising tide that lifts all boats. There's little glory in a zero-sum game, wherein for someone to win, someone must lose. Forgive the mixed metaphor, but the pie is not finite. Make a bigger pie, get everyone out of scarcity mentality, and enjoy. There are plenty of pieces to go around. Use your position to help everyone get a piece by having a seat at the table.

---

32 This is an economic theory posited by Vilfredo Pareto (1848–1923). It is also known as the "80/20 Rule."

- Have confidence. When selling yourself or something, ask why you should take this assignment or job. Ask why the company you are considering is qualified to have you. You get confidence by collecting small victories and growing. You gain confidence by working things out. You get it by learning, by earning your right to be there. Have faith in your personal agency.

- Be resilient. Fail forward. When I was in Army Basic Combat Training, the senior drill instructor encouraged us by paraphrasing William Ernest Henley's poem "Invictus": "Though your head may be bloodied, never let it be bowed."[33] It's my go-to mantra when life gets hard.

---

33 The actual Invictus passage is: "I have not winced nor cried aloud. Under the bludgeonings of chance. My head is bloody but unbowed. Beyond this place of wrath and tears."

DRESS THE PART

Perhaps an analogy to having confidence is what I call the "Frosty's Hat" phenomenon. Change the outcome by changing the action.

When a soldier chambers a round, locks, and loads a weapon, there is a mental and physical transformation from when the weapon is unloaded to when it is hot. When a weapon is hot, the soldier stands taller, breathes deeper, and is more present, situationally aware, and commanding.

You can observe the difference in civilians when they put on a suit and tie versus jeans and a T-shirt. This is the Frosty's Hat effect. In the iconic 1969 Jules Bass and Arthur Rankin Jr animation, *Frosty the Snowman*, when the old silk hat was put on Frosty, he came alive, and when the hat was off, he was not. The magic may have been in Frosty's hat, but for the rest of us, the magic is already in ourselves, and the clothes manifest it.

When developing subordinates, you can find the magic by coaching them to dress up and level up. Their demeanor and deportment will change, and they will accomplish more in their new roles as they feel better about themselves. Pro tip: Instead of a weapon, give them a clipboard and watch the magic happen.

Pay attention to patterns. Connect the dots. And when communicating, connect the dots for the listener. Just as the premise of *Don't Lead by Example* is to lead with intention, so too does that hold for communicating ideas. Don't assume the audience is tracking what you have to say. Please don't assume they will put the puzzle together the same way you intend without first showing them the picture on the box—the desired outcome.

If you've ever done dot-to-dot puzzles where you connect dots to form an image, you'll notice each dot has a number next to it, so you connect the dots with a line in the order the designer laid out. Pro tip: That's how I train by using a dot-to-dot puzzle. Take a dot-to-dot puzzle, white out the numbers next to the dots, photocopy the puzzle, and have the team connect the dots (for humorous results). Then follow it with the real puzzle. Dots are data points. Connect them and look at the emerging pattern. Spot the trend.

TAKEAWAYS

- **Sunk Costs.** What is done cannot be undone. Sunk costs are costs incurred by past actions. Since they have already occurred and cannot be recovered, they are irrelevant to future considerations. Know when to write off a relationship with a person, company, or project. Throwing good time and money after bad and hoping for a different outcome is never the answer. You see this with people who play the lottery, using the exact numbers, afraid to stop because they believe that when they do, the winning numbers will come up, and they will have lost years of investment. Another example is a car where you have replaced the transmission, then the brakes, and you don't want to get rid of it because you've put so much money into it. Let it go, Elsa, and move on.
- **Close the "Say-Do Gap."** Do what you say you're going to do when you say you're going to do it. Many procrastinate by putting off the difficult, paralyzed by *Mad How Disease*. You need to reach out for guidance and clarity well before the deliverable deadline. There is no shame in seeking

clarification. Work to eliminate the Say-Do Gap. The cure for Mad How Disease is to act *now*. Every one thing you can do now is one thing less you'll have to do later. It is not enough to know; you have to apply that knowledge. As the saying goes, "Life rewards application."

- **Know a Favor's a Favor.** People have three things to offer you: time, treasure, and talent. Their time, their money or connections, and their expertise. You can ask for one or two, but you cannot have three. Sure, ask if you need help, but do not visit that well often. People want partners, not projects. When the roles are reversed, remember 'Tis better to give than to receive, but do so to lend a hand, and expect nothing in return.

- **Embrace Reciprocity.** The healthiest relationships are reciprocal. Living intentionally is disavowing anything nonreciprocal. This includes toxic people, negative people who are energy suckers, and any personal vices like alcohol or scrolling your phone, which suck time and productivity.

- **Write for Yourself.** This book has been decades in the making, always waiting for the right time, trying hard not to offend anyone. In a conversation with God this year, the words "Write it for yourself" resonated within me. So I did, and the flood gates opened.

- **Giving Up, But Not Giving In.** Dave Ramsey says it best: "The most important decision about your goals is not what you're willing to do to achieve them, but what you are willing to give up." said Dave Ramsey. Are you willing to give up hours of scrolling, drinking, or whatever your timewasting vice of choice is to build the better you?

- **Live for Yourself.** The Stoic philosophers embraced the concept of *memento mori*, "Remember, we die." It's your life, and it will end. The first twenty to twenty-five years are when you are forming. The following fifty years are up to you. It can extend longer. It can end tomorrow, or in ten minutes. So what are you going to do?

ACKNOWLEDGMENTS

My mentors are legion. I've learned how to lead by being led by great leaders. I've also known how not to lead by being "led" or observing some not-so-great leaders. I give my thanks to those who influenced my life: God, Angie Auger, Anita S. Becker, Pat Behan, Emma Bell, Sandy Beltran, Peter Blount, Mark Bottini, Rich Brower, Tom Burton, Gerry Champagne, Connie Chang, Kristi Cruise, Deb Curran, Ed Daniels, Walter Debany, Patrick Delaney, Michael Downing, Steve Ducharme, David Durling, Erin Elliott, Karolyn Ehrenpreis, Erin Elliott, Kelsea Farrah, Logann Foltz, Mary Fosher, Christopher George, Sandy Goularte, Emily Hahn, Elizabeth Hayes, John G. Hayes Jr., Kelli Hayes, Sharon Hayes, Greg Heilshorn, Nicholas Hughes, Jamie Johnson, Rebecca Koske, Dwight Kranz, Honey Lapcharon, Karen Lynn, Malcolm Macdougall, Philip Mancuso, Charlotte McMahon, Patrick McMahon, Melinda McElheny, Caesar Meledandri, Sally Memole, Mike Mooney, Frank Morabito, Eric Morgan, Carole Murphy, Regis Murphy, Lynne Nybo, Beth Palmer, Paul Perch, Len Riggio, Patrick Robbins, Mike Rochon, Mary Sauers, Eric

Strickland, Shenandoah Titus, Natalie Thorpe, Bruce Usher, Kalani Willis, Beverly Wilson, David Yamane, Kou Yang, and so, so many more. I'm sure once this book is published, I'll slap myself on the forehead, having omitted someone unintentionally.

I want to thank Sharon Reed (Hayes) and Gail Summerskill, who lent their time and talent to editing this work before I sent it to the capable hands of Amy Ashby, Mindy Kuhn, Melissa Long, and the Warren Publishing team. It was worth the pain.

I also want to thank my children, Bennett and Nicholas, who were *voluntold* to be beneficiaries of my leadership style. And who grew up to be great men anyway.

ABOUT THE AUTHOR

Thom Hayes, has over 35 years of civilian and military leadership experience, is an entrepreneur, author and journalist. He is insatiably curious about the seemingly significant and often trivial. Thom earned the Department of Defense's Keith L. Ware Award in 2002 for Senior Writer for his coverage of the Kosovo War. He lives in Winston-Salem, NC with his wife Sharon, and a Goldendoodle named Buddy.

CPSIA information can be obtained
at www.ICGtesting.com
Printed in the USA
BVHW080424110222
628632BV00006B/939

9 781954 614901